Dark Minerva

Prolegomena: The Moral Construction of Dante's Divine Comedy

For Gaspare Finali

I0617912

Giovanni Pascoli

Translated By Richard Robinson

Sunny Lou Publishing Company
Portland, Oregon, USA
http://www.sunnyloupublishing.com

1st Edition: December 28, 2022

ISBN: 978-1-955392-35-8

* * *

This translation from Italian is based on
the Tipografia di Raff. Giusti publisher-bookseller
edition of *Minerva Oscura,* Livorno, 1898.

Contents

Letter to Gaspare Finali

Most Excellent Senator,

This study of mine was already published, although
with some variation, in the *Convito* by Adolfo de Bo-
sis, one of the noblest hearts and greatest minds that I
have had and will be permitted to have the opportunity to admire and love. In that *Convito* in which the
most elect spirits offered (with what fruit of praise
and favor, Adolfo might say) to their fellow citizens
ideal trophies fervent with generous thoughts, saying,
with the poet of Mytilene, Χαῖρε καὶ πῶ τάνδε[1] – I too
was likewise burning to offer; and I put forward,
among other things, these *Prolegomena* to the *Dark
Minerva*, as much to say the key for unlocking the
mystery of Dante. My secret and favorite task took
five or six years: I meditated on it for days entire and
dreamt about it at night (smile or laugh, you who will;
but it is true!). It was my companion, my comfort, my
pride. From the scorn which I have never known to
go without, I refuged myself in the dark *Treasury* of
my argumentations and divinations; I went over them
and repeated them, and exited from them beaming
with a solitary pride. To have peered into Dante's
thought! I often recalled the affirmation that can be
read in his *Convivio,* and which is mentioned in Chap.
III of these *Prolegomena*: "*La vera sentenza... per alcuno vedere non si può, s'io non la conto*;"[2] and I applied to the *Comedy* what he says about his convivial

---

[1] The poet of Mytilene: Alceaus (620-580 BC), a Greek lyric poet.
The phrase "Χαῖρε καὶ πῶ τάνδε" is attributed to him.

songs; and I added: "And I, I have seen it, the true meaning!" Yes: I had arrived at the *Pole* of Dante's world, that world that all scholars approach like the work of another God! I had discovered in a certain way the law of gravity of that other *Nature*; and that other nature, the laws of Dante's Universe, was ready to reveal everything to me! And in this way I concluded in our *Convito* by speaking about the *glory* that because of *research and so important a discovery* was bound to *accrue to me*.

Not two years have passed since then, and, while faith in my discovery has grown stronger than ever, every desire for glory and vainglory has vanished from my heart. If life is vanity, glory is the shadow cast by that vanity. Let us be rid of those arrogant words then! May whoever might have been scandalized pardon me! Oh! if glory is vanity's shadow, if it is the vaporization of nothing, not so vain and so small a thing is the desire for it. It is a desire to overcome, a desire to push down and vilify someone else. Be gone from my heart such perverse ferment!

And the perverse ferment has vanished, and there is nothing anymore within me except a great aspiration to contemplate and to love. So that now I am pleased to think that even in this poor work of mine I have done nothing but contemplate, with no other aim than that of contemplating. May no other benefit accrue to me than this one, to be loved by whoever contemplated, with me, the Dantesque *miro gurge*[3]; and, if by no one else, by you, great and good honor, my

---

[2]*La vera sentenza...*: Italian for "The true meaning... for those who cannot see it, if I don't relate it."

presidium; by you who know Dante as few others do; by you who write about him with such profundity of thought and such dignity of style; by you who, amidst the busy and grave cares of your high office, find courage in the good and inspiration in the truth; by you who, finally, love Dante and love (how difficult it is to say, and yet how sweet!) – you who still love me, the least interpreter of him; as much to say that you are the star that shines brightly in heaven and I am the pendulous and ephemeral water drop that reflects it here below.

You love me, illustrious senator, and I love you; and for that I dedicate to you these *Prolegomena*; not without thinking that also, in this way, I succeed in performing an act of homage to the firm ground of Romagna, which was a mother to the both of us and whose wholesomeness and geniality, whose strength and gentility, She attests to, with her ancient virtue; to that firm ground that harbored great memories and great misfortunes, Empire and Dante; not without thinking that in this way, by me, a supreme tribute of affection is offered to that dear soul in whose pious memory an indissoluble bond is established between us; to my father.

Messina, January 20, 1898.

– GIOVANNI PASCOLI.

---

[3]*Miro gurge*: Italian for "admirable maelstrom or abyss," a quote from Dante.

Prolegomena

To know and to describe Dante's thought, will it ever be possible? He eclipses in the profundity of his thought: he intentionally eclipses. I have already set my heart on following him in one of those disappearances in which, after having said "LOOK," he immediately leaves us in the dark. This time I said to myself, if I see, I will always see; if I understand him in this place, I will understand him everywhere else.

I.

The darkest passage of the *Inferno* is between cantos VII and IX inclusive. And the hour is midnight. It is midnight when the Poet descends with Virgil "*a maggior pieta;*"[4] whereas it was evening when "*apparecchiava a sostener la guerra sì del cammino e sì della pietate.*"[5] The stars fall[6] and encourage sleep: it is the hour when Aeneas with the voice we hear resonating in Virgil's verse, deep and almost hidden, prepares to narrate the last night of Troy. And Dante, who already in the evening, in the silence and universal drowsiness, felt as though he was of all living beings the only one awake; at the hour of midnight he seems oppressed by a dream he dreamt during the entirety of

---

[4]*A maggior pieta*: Italian for "to greater torment." *Inferno*, VII 97.

[5]*Apparecchiava*...: Italian for "he prepared [me] to sustain the war of both the journey and the torment." *Inferno*, II 3-4.

[6]The stars fall: *Inferno*, VII 98.

a nocturnal journey. And the journey appears to be one of those that we can remember taking as children (Dante is like a little boy beside Virgil) a short ways on foot, then carried along in a carriage, then having descended without having entirely realized it, one is jostled about here and there amidst the creaking and cracking and screeching and thuds, with some caressing words murmured into ear in the middle of a continually and deafeningly noisy ride. The Shade and the Living descend, accompanied by the sound of an assiduous gurgling from a ditch of dark water, and this ditch turns into a bog, the bog of "Sadness," at the bottom of a slope. And the bog is filled with the clamor of souls brawling amongst themselves and the bursting of bubbles that come from other souls thick in the mud. They move in a large arc along the edge and find themselves before a tower. The tower beckons by two flames on the top of it, and at a distance another person gives a signal. A boat approaches from out of the darkness, and the boatswain cries sinisterly. They board, they go. To Dante appears an enemy, now dead, covered in mud, who does not recognize him and perchance wants to climb into the boat; but he is recognized by Dante and pushed away. The midnight journey takes them through an infernal scene of hatred and contempt and just vendetta and impotent rage and fighting amongst the dead. The clamor of the damned grows distant; but then suddenly, right before them, is an immense lament, at the very bottom of a reddening fire: it is a city of incandescent iron, Dis, the real Hell. They disembark, and

for the first time Dante sees them, "*da' ciel piovuti*";[7]
for the first time he is left alone; for the first time he
sees his Teacher, eyes fixed on the ground, doubting
and sighing; he hears him uttering broken sentences
and telling a bleak story of spells and places deep and
dark within the earth. The appearance of the Furies
interrupts him, the Gorgon comes in turn, and Virgil
covers Dante's eyes with his hands. When he is thus
without sight, he hears the approach of something like
a storm. The liberator comes, a Messenger sent by
heaven who opens the iron gates with a wand. And he
reawakens finally: and Dante finds himself in a cemetery, the tombs of which are open and from which
exit flames. Between the height of danger, when the
Gorgon appears on top of the fiery tower, and his
reawakening, there is a warning to wholesome intel-
lects that seems like a flash of lightning and which
lights up the darkness suddenly, but then leaves
things darker and more inert than before. Now is the
moment when, more than ever or in any other place,
there is doubt and darkness. The Styx, the towers,
Phlegyas, Virgil's words, the Furies, the Gorgon, the
Messenger: all a mystery. But in the Styx, which en-
circles the dolorous city, "*il fummo è più acerbo*."[8]

II.

I was thinking:

    His *Comedy* required Dante to speak in a man-

---

[7]*Da' ciel piovuti*: Italian for "[those] fallen from heaven." *Inferno*,
VIII 83.

[8]*Il fummo...*: Italian for "the smoke is more biting." *Inferno*, XI 75.

ner "*faticosa e forte*"[9]; and he certainly believed as in the song "*Voi che, intendendo,*"[10] if not more so, that those who understood his thought well had to be rare, provided the beauty of it was seen, even if the goodness of it was less felt.[11] Of course, he says as much in the poem itself, both that he conceals the doctrine under the veil of verse and that his readers will need to be well versed in doctrine; of his being, that is, difficult or obscure, tiring or hard. Before the gates when the fierce Erinyes summon the Gorgon, and the Teacher covers Dante's eyes, he interrupts the story (which picks up again with clamorous din above the turbid waves), saying to the reader:

> *O voi, che avete gl'intelletti sani*
> *Mirate la dottrina che s'asconde*
> *Sotto il velame degli versi strani.*[12]

Thus, in the valley of flowers, the hymn of the compline now finished, before narrating the descent of the two angels and the advent of the serpent, he turns to the reader:

> *Aguzza qui, lettor, ben gli occhi al vero,*

---

[9]*Faticosa e forte*: Italian for "tiring and difficult." From the *Convivio*, first song, second book.

[10]*Voi che, intendendo*: Italian for "You who, hearing [me]" – the first words of the first song, second book, of *Convivio*.

[11]Original footnote: Canzone "*Voi che intendendo*", Tornata, v. 1-3 and *Convivio,* II chap XII.

[12]*O voi...*: Italian for "O you who have wholesome intellect, look at the doctrine that is hidden under the cover of strange verse." *Inferno*, IX, 61 ff.

> *Chè il velo è ora ben tanto sottile,*
> *Certo, che il trapassar dentro è leggiero.*[13]

The veil is literal, in a literal sense the exterior, and the truth is what is within hidden beneath the mantle of that tale: what is inside, a truth as he says, is hidden beneath beautiful lies.[14] The veil here is thin, the truth easily shows through then: why the admonishment to listen up? To understand this one must reread the reason, as he explains it, in the *Convivio,* for the "difficulty" or "gravity" not only of the songs, but "of the writing which can almost be called a commentary," which, designed to remove the defect of difficulty found in it, is "a bit difficult in places."[15] Dante writes that because of exile and because of the dry wind that dolorous poverty exhales, which was the effect of it, having appeared vile to many eyes, and not only in his person but in every work, those already written and to be written, he was convinced to give to the *Convivio* a little gravity and a loftier style, whereby it appears to possess greater authority.[16] Now, without wishing to take the divine author of the

---

[13]*Aguzza qui...*: Italian for "Set, reader, your eyes on the truth, in that the veil is rather thin, and arriving at it will certainly be easy." *Purgatory*, VIII 19 ff.

[14]Original footnote: *Convivio*, II 1: "peròcche in ciascuna cosa che ha 'l dentro e 'l fuori è impossibile venire al di dentro, se prima non si viene al di fuori: onde, conciossiacosachè nelle scritture la litterale sentenza sia sempre al di fuori, impossibile è venire all'altre, massimamente all'allegorica, sanza prima venire alla litterale."

[15]Original footnote: *Convivio,* I 3.

[16]Original footnote: *Convivio,* I 3, 4.

Comedy literally, one must also believe that with allegory and with the reproduction of doctrine and the subtlety of reasoning he positions himself to be more lofty than clear, more secret than accessible, more authoritative than persuasive. Admittedly, restricting the discourse to allegory one can easily see that if Jesus adopted it in the form of parables to make his divine word more easily understood, by others it was used either out of a fear of those in power in order to avoid their vengeance, or by a display of art with the intent of filling listeners with admiration. In such cases it is not the merit of clarity that is sought after by the allegorist, through which his thought might be made accessible to everyone, but the vanity of ingeniousness, in which either he partially hides the truth, so that to some people it seems very manifest but to others very occult, or he hides it from everyone so that an effort must be made to pass within. Now, when the Poet admonishes the reader to pay attention to the truth, he challenges him in a certain way, puts him to the test by indicating to him a subtle veil through which everything may be seen, even while saying that not everyone will see it; if that happens in the case of a rather thin veil, what will happen in the case of thicker covers and more unfamiliar verse?

III.

So with such words Dante warns us of the "difficulty" of his *Comedy* because of the allegory that covers his meaning; in other words he reminds us of its difficulty, for the doctrine that it is necessary to possess in order to understand:

O voi che siete in piccioletta barca,
Desiderosi d'ascoltar, seguiti
Dietro al mio legno che cantando varca,

Tornate a riveder li vostri liti:
Non vi mettete in pelago, ché forse,
Perdendo me, rimarreste smarriti.

L'acqua ch'io prendo già mai non si corse;
Minerva spira, e conducemi Apollo,
E nove Muse mi dimostran l'Orse.

Voi altri pochi che drizzaste il collo
Per tempo al pan de li angeli, del quale
Vivesi qui ma non sen vien satollo,

Metter potete ben per l'alto sale
Vostro navigio, servando mio solco
Dinanzi a l'acqua che ritorna equale.[17]

The ocean or high seas is the third Song; the little boat that was able to be of utility to those desirous of listening, in the other two parts of the Poem, no longer serves. Of course, doctrine occurred there as well, but now even more: then it was enough to listen and understand, now one must possess the doc-

---

[17]*O voi...*: The first stanzas of *Paradise*, the third book of the *Divine Comedy,* a summary of which, from Italian, is "O you who in your little boat, wishing to follow me in my ship, turn back lest I leave you behind; the water I ride on has never been sailed before, Minerva fills my sails and Apollo leads me... the few among you who hunger for the bread of Angels, continue to follow me..." *Pardise*, II 1-15.

trine oneself, so as not to be left behind when one
loses sight of the Poet's wooden ship and out of range
of his musical voice. It is inferred that the difficulty
of the third Song is not only greater than the first two,
but of a different kind: one might say that the difficulty in the former two comes from the allegory or
symbols, which are part and parcel of the poet's art,
whereas in the latter it comes more particularly from
the depth of the knowledge, which involves philosophy and theology. But, in summary, Dante himself
has confessed to a desire to be obscure and a desire
on the one hand to exercise acuity and on the other to
put his readers' doctrine to the test. And woe to the
reader if this acuity and this doctrine be merely in
quantity and quality what were needed to remove the
veil from the songs of the *Convivio*! These words
would be written, in dark letters, on the gate of the
Comedy: *La vera sentenza... per alcuno vedere non si
può, s'io non la conto.*[18]

IV.

But to hope in earnest that the sacred Poem, although
intentionally very difficult, be nevertheless accessible
to our minds, invites one consideration among several. The Poet of the *Convivio* declares that from his
Commentary the reader can derive an effect: "*non
solamente... diletto buono a udire, ma sottile am-
maestramento, e a così parlare e a così intendere
l'altrui scritture.*"[19] Now, there is no need to go on at
length to suggest that by understanding the *Comedy*

---

[18]*La vera sentenza*...: Italian for "The true meaning... cannot be
seen by anyone, if I do not reveal it." *Convivio*, I 3 to the end.

he imagined for the reader, in addition to pleasure and instruction, an effect of broader and deeper utility. The entire poem attests to us that the Poet proposed that effect as his goal, but not his principal goal I might add; because the Poet's principal goal is really this: to write poetry. But after this, Dante then proposed for himself a goal of instruction; and of how much and of what sort he does not happen to say; but that it has to be "vital" goes without saying. Now, why would he build a high wall around a fountain of life? To hope consequently that anyone who might find the way is free to do so, is reasonable. And to find it, he says, one needs to follow him, and not let him out of sight or hearing, and to force oneself to pass beyond the veil of the word, and from the outside to enter within. So I point out that in the end he who gives such warnings and counsels is, in a certain way, a different Dante from the one who first follows Virgil and then Beatrice; it is him alright, but at that moment he steps out of the admirable fiction of his song and draws our attention to it: he is no longer the actor, but the author, speaking. Now, I believe that in order for us to understand the poem we need to follow the actor, the Dante who figures in it, who is continually and gradually instructed and guided and illuminated; first by Virgil, then by Beatrice, and here and there learning from everyone and from everything; and he feigns, in order to show others how they might conduct themselves, to his having been led "out of a service... to liberty." From Dante's perspective, then, I think it is natural that no small obscurity should res-

---

[19]*Non solamente...*: Italian for "not only... [something that is] a delight to hear, but of subtle instruction, how to speak as well as how to understand others' writings."

ult, because the author, feigning that the actor is instructed in the truth as he goes along, cannot tell the truth such as it is, all in one shot; so it is to be hoped that the light goes on for us, the reader, unless we presume to precede Dante himself and to see more of what he himself says he saw.

V.

He is not the schoolboy who, narrating how he learnt, clarifies the stages of his apprenticeship into the light, which only at the end of a long discipline was made manifest to him; but the disciple who, wishing that others learn as he did, does not hide his gradual passage from ignorance to knowledge. He is not that pilgrim who narrates his journey like someone who, after long uncertainty wandering about in the darkness and half light, sees finally, in broad daylight, the way that he had not seen before when he was wandering about at night and at dawn, and describes it to others as he saw it in the light of the sun, not as he glimpsed at it in the dark or in the haze; but as someone guiding another person along a road that he himself has already travelled but which is new to the latter, and who wants to let him experience all the doubts and discomforts of the journey so as not to diminish for him the joy of arriving, after his having groped his way along; in other words, to discover for himself, after having been ignorant. He shows himself, from the very beginning, to be a diffident schoolboy and a timorous pilgrim. The outcome of the journey and of the instruction does not mean that by his telling us the story he hides from us such fear and diffidence.

Dante lets himself be led along immediately on arrival, when Virgil said that he would guide him, if for no other reason than to escape the evil of the wolf, and "worse"; but as soon as he has moved away with him, he does not want what he wanted, and Virgil, to heal him of his cowardice and fear (Dante's language would have us believe only in an influx of modesty), tells him why he came, minutely explaining to him not only that he was entreated by Beatrice, but that Beatrice was moved by Lucia, and Lucia by the Gentle Lady:

> *Dunque che è? perchè, perchè ristai?*
> *Perchè tanta viltà nel core allette?*
> *Perchè ardire e franchezza non hai?*

> *Poscia che tai tre donne benedette*
> *Curan di te nella corte del cielo,*
> *E il mio parlar tanto ben t'impromette?*[20]

Dante's flagging strength is reinvigorated, his heart is filled with ardor; but it is only Virgil's mention of the three blessed ladies that makes him return to his original purpose. Or was the "talking" not enough then, by him whom he called shortly thereafter his guide, his lord, and his teacher? No: as soon as Dante was free from imminent danger, it was no longer enough. And why? it appears that the reason is included in the prayer directed to the poet:

---

[20]*Dunque che è*...: Italian for "So, what is it? Why, why do you stand there? Why such cowardice embedded in your heart? Why do you lack daring and forthrightness? Given that three such blessed ladies who art in heaven watch over you, and my words promise you so much good?" *Inferno*, II 121 ff.

> *... Poeta, io ti richieggio*
> *Per quello Dio, che tu non conoscesti.*[21]

Dante of course realizes the fact that he who is offered to him as a savior did not know the true God; but he knows that he is (forgive the expression) the Evangelist of the acts of Aeneas and the deeds of Rome, and that he has told the story of Aeneas' descent. But he distrusts, he distrusts:

> *Tu dici, che di Silvio lo parente*
> *Corruttibile ancora, ad immortale*
> *Secolo andò, e fu sensibilmente.*[22]

With all the more asseveration he says, continuing:

> *Andovvi poi lo Vas d'elezione!*[23] [24]

Under the effect of these two extraordinary events, Dante has reason to believe them as both justified and true; and whoever knows the poet knows that the effect of the first must not have appeared less than the second to him; but, in his poetic fiction, with the attenuated phrase "*Non pare indegno ad uomo d'in-*

---

[21]*Poeta, io ti...*: Italian for "Poet, I entreat you, by that God whom you did not know." *Inferno*, I 130 ff.

[22]*Tu dici, che...*: Italian for "You tell of Aeneus who, when still alive, visited the immortal realm." Inferno, II 13 ff.

[23]Original footnote: *Inferno*, II 28.

[24]*Andovvi poi...*: Italian for "Then went he, the Vessel of election." Vessel of election, or the chosen vessel, is an epithet given to St. Paul (when Saul still) by Jesus. See Acts 9:15.

telleto"[25] and with the parenthetical "*A voler dir lo vero*,"[26] the assurance that he has does not seem certain when he says:

> *Per recarne conforto a quella fede*
> *Ch'è principio alla via di salvazione.*[27]

Nor does it escape notice after the first cry of "*Per quello Iddio che tu no conoscesti*,"[28] when he speaks after the meditation on fear and doubt, that he no longer utters the actual name of God, but circumscribes or hints at "the adversary of evil,"[29]and "someone else." But in the "words" of Virgil, when they echo other "true words," he believes more than in the earlier "talk"; and every doubt or fear he has vanishes. Forever? Quite the opposite. "Suspicion" and "cowardice" appear immediately at the ingress to hell, and he has need of the "cheerful face" of the teacher in order to feel recomforted. But Virgil's face is not always encouraging; when it turns pale, out of compassion, it is enough for Dante (whose attention is always fixed on the guide) to hesitate to descend:

> *... Come verrò, se tu paventi,*

---

[25]*Non pare...*: Italian for "It does not seem unworthy of a man of intellect." *Inferno*, II 19.

[26]*A voler dir lo vero*: Italian for "to tell the truth." *Inferno*, II 22.

[27]*Per recarne...*: Italian for "to bring back comfort from that faith which is the beginning of the way to salvation." *Inferno*, II 29 ff.

[28]*Per quello...*: Italian for "by that God that you did not know." *Inferno*, I 131.

[29]*L'avversario d'ogni male. Inferno*, II 16.

Che suoli al mio dubbiare esser conforto?[30]

The conviction inspired in him by Virgil's words, which echo Beatrice's, do not remain firm and immutable and always have need of renewed confirmation.

And in the second circle he immediately encounters what nourishes his concealed wariness, in the words of Minos:

Guarda com'entri, e di cui tu ti fide;[31]

if it weren't for the Teacher being prepared to ward off the infernal judge's insinuation, as we call it. Nor can he find encouragement in the third circle when he notices the great worm showing its teeth, not only at him, but at the both of them:

Quando ci scorse Cerbero, il gran vermo,
Le bocche aperse, e mostrocci le sanne.[32]

If he had understood that he alone was being threatened, and not Virgil, he would have trusted that he had a secure helper in him; but Virgil was equally at danger with him. It is true that even this time the Teacher is ready, no longer with words, but with fists-

---

[30]*Come verrò...*: Italian for "How shall I come, if you are afraid, you who should be a comfort to my doubt?" *Inferno*, IV 17.

[31]*Guarda com'entri...*: Italian for "Be careful as you enter, and in whom you trust." *Inferno*, V 19.

[32]*Quando ci scrose...*: Italian for "When Cerberus, that great worm, noticed us, he opened his mouth and showed us his fangs." *Inferno*, VI 22 ff.

ful of dirt. In the fourth circle, Dante's fear has time
to manifest itself, at the sound of Pluto's harsh voice;
whereupon the Teacher turns to him in order to comfort him:

> ... *Non ti noccia*
> *La tua paura, chè, poder ch'egli abbia,*
> *Non ti torrà lo scender questa roccia.*[33]

Up until now, in all four circles, Dante either
explicitly or implicitly has expressed having had fear;
which means he did not yet have perfect trust in Virgil: in the fifth circle then, his lack of trust is such that
he proposes they beat a retreat:

> *Pensa, Lettor, se io mi sconfortai*
> *Nel suon delle parole maledette;*
> *Ch'io non credetti ritornaci mai.*
>
> *O caro duca mio, che più di sette*
> *Volte m'hai sicurtà renduta, e tratto*
> *D'alto periglio che incontro mi stette,*[34]

(Actually, it was not really seven times, and
that exaggeration attests to his present fear, and the
words that follow demonstrate, as if there were any

---

[33]*Non ti noccia*...: Italian for "Do not let your fear get the best of
you, in that, although he is powerful, he will not prevent you from
descending this rock." *Inferno*, VII 4 ff.

[34]*Pensa, Lettor*...: Italian for "Think, reader, whether I was
discomforted or not by the sound of those accursed words; in that
I did not believe that I would ever return. 'O my dear duke, who
have more than seven times reassured me and saved me from
the imminent danger that beset me,'" *Inferno*, VIII 94 ff.

need for it, his past fear.)[35]

> *Non mi lasciar, diss'io, così disfatto:*
> *E se'l passar più oltre c'è negato,*
> *Ritroviam l'orme nostre insieme ratto.*[36]

Left alone for a while, Dante is in doubt; and the reasons for and against continuing on his journey wage a battle in his head; then, seeing his Lord turn back with an unusual gait, eyes to the ground, lacking in self-confidence, and sighing, he is amazed, and his cowardice makes him turn pale in the face; and to hear him speak in fits and starts he grows ever more afraid, and he admits to having greatly doubted that he could realize Virgil's hope and expectation that anyone might descend the slope from the gate of hell to there. Now, he could not be, if ever, anywhere but in the Outer Edge Limbo given that the other damned souls are reduced to the circle appropriate to their transgression; and for this reason Dante asks whether from the Outer Edge of Limbo anyone can enter into the lower circles. Virgil shows that he believes Dante's distrust is not in the expected savior but in himself; and he responds, assuring him that he has already made the journey before; and therefore:

---

[35]Editor's note: one could also imagine, so as to lend verisimilitude to the tale, incidents that Dante the pilgrim had gone through, but which Dante the poet had not (yet) related. Just as in life we are not always privy to every event that happens in another person's. See Teodolinda Barolini in her commentary on the *Divine Comedy*.

[36]*Non mi lasciar...*: Italian for "'Do not leave me,' I said, 'so undone; and if we are denied further passage, let us quickly retrace our steps.'" *Inferno*, VIII 94 ff.

Ben so il cammin: però ti fa securo.[37]

But Dante does not rest reassured, not having understood the sacred words of the messenger from heaven, but in the sixth circle he can make, in a certain manner, amends for his doubts, saying to the Teacher whom he follows docilely now ("*io dopo le spalle*"):[38]

> *O virtù somma, che per gli empi giri*
> *Mi volvi,... come a te piace.*[39]

Of course, having passed through the gates of Dis, Dante is right to believe in the Teacher, and (immediately before descending into the lower abyss) he gives proof of it, requesting a compensation from him for the time they are otherwise to lose, and receives from him a description of all Hell.

VI.

Now, how is this minute and exact description not such as to remove every difficulty that might prevent us from seeing the moral construction of Hell, and for that reason the philosophical system of the entire poem? I believe that it is due to the fact that Dante himself did not want to be clear. And why? Best to

---

[37]*Ben so il cammin...*: Italian for "rest assured: I know the passage well." *Inferno*, IX 30.

[38]*Io dopo le spalle*: Italian for "right behind him."

[39]*O virtù somma...*: Italian for "O highest virtue, you who take me round through the impious circles,... as it pleases you." *Inferno*, X 4 ff.

answer that with a question: why did Dante lack sufficient faith in, and sometimes openly doubt, Virgil?
The answer is easy: because Virgil is the symbol of
something in which we are mistaken to put our entire
and infinite trust, whether that be Reason or Philosophy; and we must trust in it only when it demonstrates
to us its being moved by those same three ladies who
are called the Gentle Lady,[40] Lucia, and Beatrice; to
our being moved by Beatrice in order to limit ourselves and go straight to Beatrice:

Con lei ti lascerò nel mio partire.[41]

Now, if the philosophical exposition of the
guilt punished in Hell is not clear to us, we may fun-
damentally believe that it is not clear precisely because it is made by someone who could not make it
clear. To which we may add that, even if he could,
Virgil would not have made a complete clarity of it
because he is the Teacher, and the Teacher must make
the disciple figure it out. In proof of which two
points, I allude to what Virgil himself says in *Purgatory*, in the description he makes of Purgatory, in
verse 139 of the XVIIth canto for the second point,
and to verses 46-49 of the XVIIIth canto for the first.
From these last verses we may conclude that Virgil
can give only "what reason sees here."[42] And what
did reason see then in the organization and division of

---

[40]Gentle Lady: the Holy Mother Virgin Mary.

[41]*Con lei ti...:* Italian for "With her I will leave you when I depart."
Inferno, I 123.

[42]*Quanto ragion qui vede. Purgatory* XVIII 46.

sins in Hell? It saw what had been taught by the teacher of those who know, whose *Ethics* and *Physics* are cited.[43] We may add to that the book *De Officiis* by Cicero, which Dante had either read in its entirety or knew only some extracts of.

VII.

What must we conclude about the "moral construction" of Hell? About the division of sins?[44] This: that of the three dispositions that Heaven does not want, the first, Incontinence, is punished outside the burning-red city, and that the other two, Malice and mad Bestiality, within it; that the latter two are equivalent then to a triple Malice, whose end is abuse; the three kinds of Malice are Violence, Fraud in which trust is not involved, Fraud in which trust is involved or someone "who betrays." Can anyone in fact maintain that mad Bestiality is different from this triple Malice. Of Incontinence, there are of course three sins which Dante, the disciple of Virgil, already knows the names of: the carnal sin or vice of lust (V 38 and 55) of those whom the wind buffets; the sin of gluttony (VI 53) of those whom the rain batters; the avarice (VII 48) or prodigality (42) or niggardliness or spendthriftiness (58) of those whom one meets with such biting tongues. Does he know even the name perhaps of the sin of those in the fertile bog? In it are the souls of those whom anger overcame (VII 116), and also the sad souls who carry within themselves

---

[43]Whose *Ethics* and *Physics*... are cited: Two works by Aristotle.

[44]Original footnote: *Inferno*, XI 16-111.

apathetic vapors (121). The sin is therefore twofold and contrary, as with those of the fourth circle: anger and sloth. Nothing clearer can be said at this point: now, how is obscurity or incompleteness spoken about? Oh! so obscure and incomplete is Virgil's exposition of it. Leaving aside the point about mad Bestiality, which I have never understood how it could raise doubts or disputes, and reducing to a few words the large amount that has been written on the subject, how is it possible that of the seven capital sins, Envy and Pride are not punished in the Dante's *Inferno*? Or are they punished but under another name and under another system, within Dis, where Envy and Pride would have their punishment alongside Ire, Lust, Greed or, what do I know, something more serious than those within the first circle and the Styx? But why would these, if they are minor sins, have a place assigned to them outside Dis, while Pride and Envy here and there have a place assigned to them only within Dis? The answer is not: they are more serious; because, of that gradation this side of Dis whereby Lust is less serious than Gluttony, and Gluttony than Avarice, and Avarice than Ire and Sloth, it can no longer be discovered whether, for example, Brunetto is lustful or, for example, Azzolino is irascible. And so the other two sins would be found with these five. But it may also be that these two sins are found in the Styx, barely alluded to by an adjective or hinted at by an attitude or behavior. That may also be; but then if that were true I would always need to conclude, just as I conclude believing something else altogether, that Virgil's teaching is obscure, or that reason, although illuminated by Aristotelian philosophy, does not see enough, or that the Teacher wants to train the disciple and habituate him to work things out on his own, or all these things. Naturally, Virgil himself makes known the insufficiency of philosophical lights when he cites, if only to confirm an idea by Aristotle, a book of a completely different nature than either *Ethics* or *Physics* ("your" *Ethics*, "your" *Physics,* one notes): Genesis.

VIII.

Useful and necessary is it to turn to the other lesson that Virgil gives to Dante, in Purgatory, with respect to its order or arrangement. I observe that, while in Hell Virgil reasoned in particular detail about the three large circles that they had yet to see, in Purgatory he keeps quiet about how it is threefold Love that is wept for in the three circles above them:

> *L'amor ch'ad esso troppo s'abbandona,*
> *Di sopra noi si piange per tre cerchi;*
> *Ma come tripartito si ragiona,*
>
> *Tacciolo, acciocchè tu per te ne cherchi.*[45]

Now, in these three circles is espied Avarice, Gluttony, Lust, the which sins are punished in Hell, not in the three large circles that were yet to be visited, but in the three already visited before the Styx. There is in this a correspondence, a strange one, I will

---

[45]*L'amor ch'ad esso*...: Italian for "Love which abandons itself too much to this, is wept for in the three circles above us; But how it is divided into three parts, I keep quiet, so that you might work it out for yourself." *Purgatory*, XVII 136 ff.

say, given that in Hell one speaks about what remains
to be seen and keeps quiet, for starters, about what
has been seen, whereas in Purgatory, on the contrary,
what is seen is spoken about, and what remains to be
seen, at least in part, is kept quiet about. And what remains to be seen is located above the speakers in Purgatory, but below them in Hell, and what has been
seen is just the opposite. But there is also a correspondence that is less material and local; in that in Purgatory Virgil does not give a particular definition of the
three sins that are lamented above them, and lets
Dante work it out on his own, while in Hell Dante had
very clearly remembered the same three sins: "*Quei...
Che mena il vento e che batte la pioggia e che s'in-
contran con sì aspre lingue*,"[46] that is, the carnal sinners, the kings of the offenses of gluttony, the kings
of prodigality. To which are to be added those of the
fertile bog, that is, those whom anger wins over and
who carry apathetic vapors within themselves. Would
it not seem that the Poet wanted us, as Virgil wanted
him, to declare only what was necessary, passing over
what was not? Now then, declaring more minutely in
Purgatory the three sins of Avarice, Gluttony, and
Lust was not necessary? It was not, and in fact it is
something understood by everyone, just as that threefold love is reasoned about. Why? In the economy of
the poem it can only be because Dante with respect to
Virgil, and we with respect to Dante, any doubts we
had are clarified by having already seen those same
three sins of incontinence in Hell, and by having also
learnt their names. And only for this does Virgil as-

---

[46]*Quei... Che mena...*: Italian for "Those... whom the wind buffets
and whom the rain batters and who are met with such biting
tongues." *Inferno*, XI 70-72.

sign that light task to Dante, as if to say: Oh! let us
see whether the journey through eternity bears fruit!
Let us see whether you remember both what you have
seen and what I have said to you. Now, if Virgil
leaves it to Dante to recognize these three sins because they are easy to recognize, the others which he
himself gives signs and definition of, they would not
seem so easily recognizable. And why? because they
were not seen in Hell where Dante lacks experience
and instruction? Maybe; however no one could forget
having seen their anger; but it may also be because
now it is discussed more clearly, whereas earlier it
was spoken about obscurely. And, accepting for a
moment this last supposition, we would find all of a
sudden that first correspondence that I mentioned be-
coming clearer and enlightening us: both explanations
have a part that is clear, the first, and a part that is obscure, the second; the first, which regards what has
been seen, the second, what remains to be seen; but
because they are in inverse order respectively, the
part that is clear of the first explanation casts its light
on the dark part of the second, and the clear part of
the second casts its light on the dark part of the first.
And that would lead us to this: like Dante, having
heard those guilty of incontinence defined as sinners
of the flesh or lust, guilty of gluttony, damned for
prodigality, he could easily recognize those who
throughout the three circles wept for the love that one
too greatly abandons himself to for what does not
make men happy; thus, having understood now in
Purgatory that the proud, the envious, and the irascible were expiating the tripartite love of evil, he must
have concluded, after thinking about the explanations

he had heard in Hell, that the sinners of the three large
circles, perpetrators of malice, whose end is injury
and who can be divided into three types according to
whether the injury is made with force or by fraud or
by betrayal, – they were precisely the hot-tempered,
the envious, and the proud. But since it is premature
to draw a conclusion, let us hold this for certain: that
the two explanations regard seven divisions of sinners: the first four having already been seen,

> *... quei della palude pingue,*
> *Che mena il vento and che batte la pioggia*
> *E che s'incontran con sì aspre lingue.*[47]

and three as yet to be seen in the three large circles;
the second three having already been seen, the perpetrators of the tripartite love of evil, and four as yet to
be seen, those guilty of listless love and the love that
one too greatly abandons oneself to; so that, in summary, the one realm has four sins behind and three
before, and the other has four before and three behind: and that it is without a doubt that three out of
the seven sins are common to both explanations. Nine
are the rings of hell, but the sins that Virgil reasons
about are seven. Seven and no more, seven like those
in *Purgatory*.

IX.

So it is not absurd to maintain thus far that the lesson
of Hell leaves them something to meditate on, on
their descent. Does that include Purgatory? No; and

---

[47]ibid.

from this we can confirm our opinion about that of Hell. Purgatory is not included; and this time (for what other reason than that Virgil will no longer accompany the schoolboy after Purgatory is visited?), this time Virgil admonishes Dante:

> ... *Quanto ragion qui vede*
> *Dirti poss'io; da indi in là t'aspetta*
> *Pure a Beatrice, ch'opera è di fede.*[48]

That this be something that reason cannot see and that only Beatrice can speak to is hinted at a little later on when, after having discoursed on the "*virtù che consigilia, che dell'assenso de' tener la soglia*,"[49] which is a cause of merit in us, he concludes:

> *La nobile virtù Beatrice intende*
> *Per lo libero arbitrio, e però guarda*
> *Che l'abbi a mente, s'a parlar ten prende.*[50]

And Beatrice in truth speaks with him about it in Paradise (V 19) in order to affirm the nobility of that virtue, which is the greatest gift that God gave to man. However, we know that in Dante there was a doubt; a doubt that goes back more to Virgil's words

---

[48]*Quanto ragion qui vede*...: Italian for "How much reason sees here, I can tell you; beyond that you'll need to wait for Beatrice, which is an act of faith." Purgatory, XVIII 46 ff.

[49]*Virtù che consiglia*...: Italian for "[innate within you is the] virtue that counsels, and it must keep the threshold of assent." *Purgatory*, XVIII 62-63.

[50]*La nobile virtù*...: Italian for "By noble virtue, Beatrice means free will, so keep it in mind if she speaks with you about it." *Purgatory*, XVIII 73 ff.

than to those of Beatrice; when he says

> *Quest'è il principio, là onde si piglia*
> *Ragion di meritare in voi.*[51]

Dante does not doubt that we do not have the faculty to receive and watch over both good and guilty loves; no; the philosophical explanation satisfies him, and he does not ask anything else of Virgil. But what he might have asked Virgil about in vain, and which he does not speak about, is something outside this freedom to receive and watch over, being beyond philosophy and human reason. Everyone has free will, and for that reason the opportunity to earn merit: now, how is it that some, and many in fact, receiving all the good love, will not succeed and do not succeed in earning merit? This is the doubt that Dante confesses to have conceived, according to the poetic fiction, for the reasoning put forward by Virgil, who cautions as to his inability to say just how much reason can see:

> *... il gran digiuno*
> *Che lungamente m'ha tenuto in fame,*
> *Non torvangogli in terra cibo alcuno.*[52]

It is something that Dante has no need to express: the Eagle releases him and then reveals it to him:

---

[51] *Quest'è il principio...*: Italian for "This is the principle, whence the cause of merit in you." *Purgatory*, XVIII 64 ff.

[52] *Il gran digiuno...*: Italian for "great fast that has kept me hungry for many a long season, not finding any sustenance on earth." *Paradise*, XIX 25 ff.

... tu dicevi: Un uom nasce alla riva
Dell'Indo, e quivi non è chi ragioni
Di Cristo, nè chi legga, nè chi scriva;

E tutti I suoi voleri ed atti buoni
Sono, quanto ragione umana vede,
Senza peccato in vita o in sermoni.

Muore non battezzato e sena fede;
Ov'è questa giustizia che il condanna?
Ov'è la colpa sua, s'egli non crede?[53]

Dante's doubt is resolved. I do not have to observe anything else, other than that this response by
the Eagle to the disciple's imagined question is made
when he still has to ascend to the three spheres, Saturn, the fixed Stars, the Prime Mover; not counting
the Empyrean, which includes them all. So in Hell,
after Virgil's description, Dante has three large circles
to visit. And although Hell has nine rings, we have
seen how between it and Purgatory, which has seven
ledges, there is an exact proportion of parts. It would
not seem then that such intentional correspondence
were compromised by the number of nine spheres.
Nine, I repeat, are the rings in Hell, but in his description Virgil speaks only of seven sins. And in truth, in
Christian philosophy the number of sins were reduced

---

[53]*Tu dicevi...*: Italian for "You said: a man is born on the bank of
the Indus, and there is no one there who can bear witness to
Jesus, or who reads or writes about him; And all his desires and
good deeds are, inasmuch as human reason sees, without sin in
life or in speech. He dies unbaptized and without faith; how is this
justice that condemns him? Where is his guilt if he does not
believe?" *Paradise*, XIX 70-8.

to seven. In Purgatory, Virgil reduces them for only one reason: the love that errs for either a bad object or too little or too much vigor in the pursuit of a good object. The love that errs for a bad object generates three sins: pride, envy, anger; that which errs for too little vigor, one: acedia; that which errs for too much, three as well: avarice, gluttony, lust. This is not the order that sins have in St. Thomas (*Summa*, 2nd LXXXIV 7). The order of sins in Dante are found in St. Bonaventure (*Comp.* III 14), in Hugo of Saint Victor (*All. in Matthaeum* II, XV & ff., *Institutiones Monasticae*, XXXVIII), in St. Gregory (*Mor.* XXXI 31). For what reasons are these sins thus distributed in Theologies and Dante? But in Dante were they really distributed and arranged thus? In Purgatory there was no doubt; but in Hell? Of the seven sins of Hell, what was their reason and nature? Of three, I knew the answer: of the other four, no.

X.

I said: Let us examine these four obscure sins one by one. And let us begin with the last one, with that of the ninth circle. The emperor of the dolorous kingdom is there. – How did you fall from heaven, Lucifer, you who rose in the morning?... You even said in your heart, "I will rise in heaven, I will place my throne above the stars of God, I will sit on the mountain of the Testament, on the septentrional slopes. I will ascend above the clouds, I will be like the Almighty": and yet you were dragged down to Hell, into the depths of the lake (Isaiah 14:12). – There was no doubt for me, nor for anyone else, that the first sin of the Angel was none other than pride (*Summa*, 1ˢᵗ, LXIII 2). What could the beginning of malevolence be, asks St. Augustine (*City of God*, XIV 21), if not pride? In fact, pride is the desire for perverse excellence (*City of God*, XVI 13), it is love of primacy. And because God is the greatest and first, pride constitutes rebellion to him. This then was clear to me as to everyone, that Lucifer was proud, pride itself even. But because that is the beginning of every sin (*Ecclesiasticus* 10:15), I could with others believe that Lucifer was at the bottom [of every sin], as the origin of evil. And thus did I believe. But meanwhile I put this question to myself: How is pride the origin of every sin? Doctor of the Church, St. Thomas Aquinas answered me; after having taught me that in each act of sin there is a turning toward a commutable good and a turning away from an immutable good which is God, he affirmed that in pride the turning away from God did not come from ignorance or weakness or desire for any one thing, as with other sins, but from that "*quod non vult Deo et eius regulae subiici*"[54] (*Summa*, 1ˢᵗ of the 2ⁿᵈ, LXXXIV 2). In this way every sin begins with pride, or rather with a disrespect for that law of God, which prohibits such an act. But if there is pride in every sin, there is also a pride in and of itself; if other sins, according to Boethius, run away from God, pride alone stands its ground before God. And thus in truth Lucifer is the most beautiful of Angels, who raised his eyebrows at his maker, as did the Giants, who tested their strength against the supreme Jove. Whence the one and the others really seemed to

---

[54]*Quod non vult...*: Latin for "which does not want God or [to be] subjected to his rule."

me proper symbols of pride. But if Lucifer's pride expressed itself by the raising of his eyebrows against
God, and that of the Giants with going to blows with
Jove, how, I asked, does the pride of men express itself according to the Fathers, the Doctors of the
Church, and Dante? Certainly by standing its ground
before God, with no intention of subjecting itself to
him or to his rule. But given such rules consist in
many laws and precepts such that whoever violates
them commits this or that sin, which is affected by a
pride, but is not pride, I saw that I was unable make
headway in my research, if I did not reduce all these
laws and precepts to one law and to one precept only,
which was the rule of God for Man, such that he who
violated it was a perpetrator of pride and of no other
sin. Now, as this rule, for the newly created Angel,
consisted only in this, that of recognizing God's creation and waiting for the light, (*Paradise*, XIX 48)
and he did not recognize it, and he did not wait for
him, and fell, so for Man it was time that he was reduced to the single prohibition of the apple. Why was
breaking such a prohibition, as everyone affirms,
pride? Because the Tempter said to Eve: "God knows
that on the day you eat this, your eyes will open and
you will be like Gods, knowledgable of both good
and evil"? Whence the Poet said

> *... là dove ubbidia la terra e il cielo,*
> *Femmina sola, e pur testè formata,*
> *Non sofferse di star sotto alcun velo.*[55]

---

[55]*Là dove ubbidia...*: Italian for "there where earth and heaven
obeyed, Woman alone, and only just created, did not suffer to
remain under any veil." *Purgatory*, XXIX 25.

XI.

St. Augustine responded to my questions (*City of God*, XIV 12 ff.). He responded that they were craving for a false primacy; given that a false primacy is to leave what the soul must adhere to as its Principle and in a certain way make itself be the Principle unto itself. He responded that the proud act consisted in transgressing the one precept, which demonstrated their dependence on God. He responded, "*tam leve praeceptum ad observandum, tam breve ad memoria retinendum... tanto maiore iniustitia violatum est, quanto faciliore posset observantia custodiri.*"[56] Now, this admirable comment must explain pride, it seems to me, as it was found in the first parents, and so in their children. One phrase in particular persuaded me, which at the very beginning seemed almost to have escaped Virgil in his Aristotelian explanation and almost to have been put to the side, and for which, immediately afterwards, showed itself to me to be full of illuminating power through Dante's thought: *Genesis*. Virgil, after having brought to Dante's attention the Stagirite's *Ethics* and then *Physics,* concluded his discourse by recalling that book of Holy Scripture in order to complete his treatment of the three dispositions that Heaven does not want. The book of Genesis then, as it was useful in demonstrating the way "of the usurer," could in this way serve to expose all the rest of it as well. Let us dig into that then. Adam and Eve were perpetrators of pride; because of their violating

---

[56]*Tam leve*...: Latin for "the precept being so easy to observe, and so short to remember... the violation was all the greater, given the observance was all the easier." St. Augustine, *City of God*, Book XIV, section 12.

the one prohibition given to them by God, they put themselves directly in front of him and denied all his authority and wanted to become both Principle and Rule unto themselves; and given the prohibition was very easy to observe, they transgressed a precept that, once violated, could not be excused by any imagination of justice (*City of God*, XIV 13). Now, as a result of that first sin, the prohibitions multiplied for men; it is no longer the case now of finding that one and only sin, by violation of which Man puts himself directly against God; but it is not difficult to find what is so easy to observe, which if not observed cannot be excused in any manner. The prohibitions and commandments of God given to men are contained in the Decalogue, of which the last one is "Thou shalt not covet thy neighbor's donkey," and the first of which is "Thou shalt have no other gods before me." Now, of these precepts of justice, which one is, or which are, the one violated with the greatest injustice? Clearly that or those which can be most easily observed through obedience. And so, those whose observance is more difficult are violated with less injustice. And what is more difficult than to keep one's heart from desire? From one's desire for the servant, for the female servant, for the ox, for the ass, or for "any thing that is thy neighbor's." It appears that the last prohibition was made to demonstrate that whoever will observe, in addition to the others, this so difficult precept as well, must be considered perfect; and that he who gradually violates the others is progressively less virtuous and just, so that in the end by violating the first he is completely wicked and impious.

XII.

This then I had firmly in mind when, reading in St. Thomas Aquinas, I saw that there was something neglected in my research as to the gradations among the single prohibitions and commandments, and that there was to be expected a broader and more general division between the precepts of the first Tablet and those of the second, in accordance with the dilection of God and one's neighbor. The first three are of the first, the other seven are of the second; but of these last, the first precept, "Honor thy father and thy mother: that thy days may be long upon the land which the LORD thy God giveth thee," is placed (2nd of the 2nd, CXXII 5) "immediately after the precepts that are prescribed for God, because our parents are the particular Origin of our being, as God is the Origin of the universe. Whence there is a strong affinity of that precept to those of the first Tablet." Moreover, this precept, – being distinct from the first three in that it has to do with acts of *pietas*, which is the second part of *iustitia*, while the first and main one has to do with *religio*, whose acts the first three are concerned with, – is also distinct from the last six because they are given with respect to *iustitia communiter dicta*[57], which is among equals (2nd of the 2nd, CXXII 1). So that I could distinguish the precepts of Justice in four of them, which are acts of Religion and Piety, and six of them which are acts of Justice proper. I concluded then that such precepts of Religion and Piety were those that can be observed with an easier obedience, and for that reason they are violated with greater in-

---

[57] *Iustitia communiter dicta*: Latin for "justice commonly so called."

justice. It was in this way that I set out then to recognize that it was quite possible that Dante, according to Augustine's or Aquinas' doctrine, called those men proud who, similar to Adam and Eve, had violated the precepts that, once violated, could not be excused with any imagination of Justice, and that those precepts belonged more to the first Tablet plus the fourth which is similar to them. Whoever does not recognize the Principle, both universal and particular, of our being, puts himself all the more directly in opposition to God, and because he transgresses what was the only sin for his first Parents, and for their children the least, he makes himself Principle and Rule unto himself, craving a false primacy. And I thought of the lake at the center of the earth, the lake that freezes over by the fanning of the six wings of the first proud one. It is easy to understand how I noticed immediately that it was divided into four circumscriptions, and how I recalled the four precepts of Religion and Piety, the violation of which I believed to be pride. To be honest, the lightest of the four gradations of guilt, which is punished in Caina, was rather similar to the violation of the fourth precept which, as the commandment to honor one's parents, implies also blood relatives (2nd of the 2nd, CXXII 5). But as the Doctors of the Church add the fatherland as well, and the violator of the fatherland is punished in the second circumscription which is Antenora, I imagined that either the relationship I saw was not between the four bands and the violation of the four precepts, or that Dante had seen in the sanctification of the Sabbath, which is the third precept, a deeper meaning than what we see. In truth, says St. Thomas Aquinas (2nd of

the 2nd, CXXII 4): "In the third precept of the Decalogue there is the commandment against the external
worship of God,[58] under the sign of common benefit,
which pertains to everyone, in other words it repre-
sents the act of creating the world, after which, it is
said, God rested on the seventh day." And he adds
that he imagines, anagogically, the tranquility of enjoying God, who will be in the fatherland. And to the
objection that, as with the Sabbath, one needed to
make mention also of other sacred gods and sacred
places and vessels and the like, he responds: "*observatio sabbati est signum generalis beneficii, scilicet
productionis universae creaturae.*"[59] So to celebrate
God's day of Rest is as much to recognize that God
made "*caelum et terram,*"[60] which Earth then is our
present fatherland, and Heaven our future fatherland.
And it appeared to me not impossible that, in the
symbolizing thought of the Poet, the sin of Bocca, for
example, would be expressed with these words: He
transgressed God's Sabbath. And in the case of Alberigo he could express himself with these other
words: He used the name of God in vain; because
with the second precept, the purjury that belongs to ir-
religiosity is prohibited (2nd of the 2nd, CXXII 3), and
he who violates the sanctity of the altar perjures most
seriously, according also to antiquity: "You violated
the great oath, the salt and the altar." But it was not

---

[58]External worship of God: "Thou shalt have no other gods before
me... No graven images or likenesses."

[59]*Observatio...*: Latin for "observation of the Sabbath is a sign of
general favor, in other words, of the creation of the universe."

[60]*Caelum et terram*: Latin for "heaven and earth."

necessary to continue down this path, in that it appeared to me that Dante could have in mind a simpler distinction, suggested to him by one writer whom he certainly had in mind, Cicero (*De Off.* III 10), who about Romulus the murderer of his brother had said: "*Omisit hic et pietatem et humanitatem.*"[61] And I was thinking that in any case it could be more simply affirmed that it was pride to violate Piety, as is found in Cicero, and that it was another sin altogether to violate Humanity. But here all of a sudden I stopped, saying to myself: why am I looking at these details when perhaps I was wrong on the principal point? Actually, pride is what I call the offense that is punished in the Ice; reasoning appeared to lead me directly to it. And there is something else: each of those sinners keeps his face looking down, other people as well and everyone looking down, exposed to the harm of passing feet, and still others, shades, are covered all over with frost, and Judas has his head inside a mouth of Lucifer, and Brutus and Cassius have their heads down; all fitting attitudes for the proud who are punished. There is this, and there is something else; but everything can be explained differently from how I felt the need to explain it myself. Because I was thinking of Pride, but Dante had said that there below was every sort of betrayal, and in that lake the fraudulent were punished, those who had betrayed the trust placed in them.

---

[61]*Omisit...*: Latin for "He lacked piety and a sense of humanity."

XIII.

Very good: but I had concluded that pride violates the precept of Justice and specifically those contained in the first Tablet, more than a quarter of the commandments. So I needed diligently to examine what Justice was: it is defined as follows: *"perpetua et constans voluntas ius suum uniquique tribuendi"* (2nd of the 2nd, LVIII 1);[62] and it is always applied *"ad alterum"* (ib., 2);[63] and an act of this is *"reddere unicuique quod sum est"* (ib., 1).[64] Now, if the goal of Justice is to give to each his own *"ius,"*[65] the goal of Injustice will be *"inferre iniuriam"*[66] on another. And Virgil says (*Inf.*, XI 22) that in every [act of] malice... Injury is the goal. From which one may see that malice is, in Dante, like what is termed *"kakia"* in Aristotle (*Eth.*, VII 1), like what is called *"iniustitia"* in Cicero (*De off.*, I 7, 23). Cicero, then, whom Dante had in mind more than any other author, in that canto, as being a Latin, and whom Virgil must have been familiar with more than any other writer almost, – Cicero says (ib., 13, 41): *"Cum... duobus modis, id est aut vi aut fraude, fiat iniuria"*[67]... And Dante: *"ed ogni fin co-*

---

[62]*Perpetua et constans...*: Latin for "a perpetual and constant will bestowing on each person his right."

[63]*Ad alterum*: Latin for "to another [person]."

[64]*Reddere unicuique quod suum est*: Latin for "to give to each his own."

[65]*Ius*: Latin for "right" as conferred by law.

[66]*Inferre iniuriam*: Latin for "to inflict harm."

tale O con forza o con frode altrui contrista."[68] Let's take a look at Cicero again (ib., 7, 23): "*Fundamentum... est iustitiae fides*"[69]: which, when lacking, it is clear that there will be injustice or malice, as Dante says; but especially, in Dante's thinking, that which aims to harm by fraud, or to perpetrate an evil act by deceit. And harm by fraud is of two types and constitutes, when performed, two sins of greater and lesser gravity, depending on how a man employs it against another man "'*n lui fida Ed in quei che fidanza non imborsa.*"[70] Practicing deceit on someone who has no reason to trust, breaks, according to Dante, "*Pur lo vinco d'amor che fa natura*"[71]; deceit done on someone who trusts in the other person violates both natural love and "*quel ch'è poi aggiunto Di che la fede spezial si cria.*"[72] Which brings us back to saying that the fraudulent are criminals against Justice commonly so called, while a person who betrays a trust placed in him offends both Religion and Piety; while "between

---

[67]*Cum... duobus modis...*: Latin for "Whereas... harm is done in two ways, that is, by force or by fraud."

[68]*Ed ogni...*: Italian for "And every suchlike purpose afflicts others by either force or fraud."

[69]*Fundamentum...*" Latin for "Faith [or trust] is the basis of justice."

[70]'*n lui fida...*: Italian for "who trusts in him, And who puts no trust in him." *Inferno*, II 53-54.

[71]*Pur lo vinco...*: Italian for "The very bond of love made by nature." ib., II 56.

[72]*Quel ch'è poi...*: Italian for "that which is subsequently added, which faith strengthens." ib., 62-63.

the parts of Justice which are both Religion and Piety,
and Justice commonly so called, there is this difference, that participants of the first have a debt toward
some particular people, to whom a man is obliged for
some special reason, and in the case of Justice commonly so called a man has a debt common to all." (2ⁿᵈ
of the 2ⁿᵈ, CXXII 6). Whence it follows that in Dante
betrayal does not take its quality from deception,
which is accompanied by harm, but from the person
against whom the injury is committed, the person
against whom every injury is a deception because of
that person's trust. As much to say then that there is a
betrayal, and to say that fraud is employed by the one
who is trusted in, by some special advantage he was
given, whereby a special motive of trust is created,
and to say that he offends the precepts of Religion
and Piety which command love toward God and one's
Parents; and to say with Cicero that *omisit pietatem*,[73]
and to say that he is guilty of pride. And so did it appear to me, considering the sinners of the ninth circle
and their sins, because among those who are in the
three mouths of Lucifer, Judas had directly betrayed
the Christ, and Brutus and Cassius had directly betrayed the Monarchy, which has a direct dependence
on God (*Mon.*, III 15): they had betrayed, not so
much, as I said, through fraudulent means put into action by the one and the others, but through their person because God was their benefactor, either immediately as the Christ, or mediately as Caesar; and for
this reason God and Caesar had a particular reason to
trust them, so that the Christ exclaimed: "With a
kiss!"; and Caesar, "You too, son?" Other sinners in

---

[73] *Omisit pietatam*: Latin for "he lacked piety."

Judecca and Ptolomea had also betrayed God, in the persons of those who had benefited the most by God and those who because of God were received at the hospitable altar, and both the ones and the others had for that reason complete trust in the beneficiary and in the guest. And also those of Antenora had offended God directly, which, more than anything else, I understood by the difference between Bocca, the traitor of the Guelph party or the fatherland, and Camicion de' Pazzi, the murderer of his kinsman. Because the latter does not shrink from giving his name, for he does not believe his sin is very serious compared to others, he is in fact waiting for another kinsman of his who is guilty of having betrayed the fatherland, which makes his betrayal of a relative appear less serious. Indeed, pride being an appetite for perverse excellence, such appetite cannot be shown except by whoever wants to be superior to the Almighty, that is to God. Now, this appetite is punished in Hell, as is the desire for its opposite, as Bocca clearly says to Dante, who had asked him if he wanted fame – "*del contrario ho io brama*,"[74] – and as the other sinners in the Ice clearly demonstrate. And I was thinking that what Virgil says to Antaeus regarding fame, "*Questi può dar di quel che qui si brama*,"[75] was not said because Virgil had in mind the other sinners in Hell, who are desirous of being remembered still in the gentle world, but because he knew that he was in the circle of those who had coveted celsitude, "*cui si deve*

---

[74]*Del contrario...*: Italian for "I have just the opposite desire." *Inferno*, XXXII 94.

[75]*Questi...*: Italian for "He can give you what you want here." *Inferno*, XXXI 125.

onore e reverenza"[76] (1st of 2nd, LXXXIV 2), among that supreme rank, symbolized by the words of the Angel, "*Simile sarò all'Altissimo*,"[77] and by the words of the Serpent, "*Sarete come Iddii*."[78] And the poet had made full use of, in this place, its circumscription so that the reader might understand consequently that the love of fame in terrestrial life became in Hell a great horror of it. It seemed remarkable to me that while among the sinners Camicion de' Pazzi didn't show as much disgust for renown as others in the inner rings did; that among the Giants Antaeus responded quickly to the incantation of fame. Given that Antaeus had not directly lifted a finger against the Gods, for that reason he was absolved; and so Camicion had not placed himself directly above God; but the one had been proud in that he had fought against the demigod Hercules, although it had not been a full-scale war; and the other had been guilty with respect to relatives, of that crime which is contained under the offense to the particular Principle of our being, not really to the universal Principle.

XIV.

Thus was I confirmed in my thinking, and I made many other considerations, nor did I neglect to explain to myself how and why the count Ugolino eagerly gave his name, even though he was in Antenora;

---

[76]*Cui si deve...*: Italian for "to whom one owes honor and reverence."

[77]*Simile...*: Italian for "I will be like the Almighty."

[78]*Sarete come Iddii*: Italian for "You will be like unto Gods."

but I was looking for manifest proof, which would permit me to cease having any doubt in my mind, so that I could move on: and I found it. Yes: in the Ice, pride was truly punished, which was hidden under the name of betrayal or the fraud in which one put one's trust. Both were pride, and nothing but pride, and Dante had said it so clearly as to leave no doubt. I read it, as if drunk, in St. Augustine (*City of God*, XIV 13): "It is good to lift up one's heart; not however towards oneself, which is pride; but towards the Lord, which is obedience, and which only the humble can have. Now, there appears to be something marvelous in that humility, something that lifts the heart up, and something in that elation that pulls the heart down. It appears then to be a conundrum, that elation should pull down, and humility lift up." That is why, I said, the sinners in the Ice keep their heads down, besides their being in the lowest circle. But that was not something new to me, nor to others. St. Augustine went on to explain how the humble were exalted and the proud were brought low, and he said: "It happens as it was written: 'You have beaten them down, while they were rising up.' Which is not to say: 'Because they were exalted'" almost as if they had first risen and then were beaten down again; but "While they were rising up," then they were beaten down. And he concluded: "*Ipsum... extolli iam deici est.*"[79] And you, Dante, had said of the traitors, in fact you had showed, the same thing, making them, in this way, similar to the first proud one and to the first relatives who were proud. O how not to believe that the traitors

---

[79]*Ipsum... extolli...*: Latin for "Their very exaltation was their undoing." *City of God*, 14:13

were proud, if what happens in the first also happens
in the second? And it happens: you had made Fra Alberigo say it:[80]

> *Sappi che tosto che l'anima trade,*
> *Come fec'io, il corpo suo l'è tolto*
> *Ad un demonio...*
>
> *Ella ruina in sì fatta cisterna*[81]

Just as Isaiah says about Lucifer: "*ad infernum detra-
heris in* profundum laci."[82] And why does Dante,
against every theological verisimilitude, put this fall-
en soul in Hell as soon as he betrays, unless to signify
that his betrayal is an act of pride, and that "*ipsum extolli iam deiici est*"? Just as Lucifer in the first moment of his creation was good, but in the second he
was evil (1st, LXIII 6), and as soon as he had sinned,
he was thrown down; like Adam and Eve, as soon as
they had eaten the apple, they knew their nakedness,
and they were punished; in the same way, the proud
man, as soon as he has committed that particular sin
of pride, equivalent to that of the first Angel and the
first Man, he has his eternal damnation. Because the
traitor in Dante is considered to "*aderire immobili-
mente al male che appetì,*"[83] as Aquinas (1st, LXIV 2)
says of the sinning Angel. In this way I was left think-

---

[80]Original footnote: *Inferno*, XXXIII 129 ff.

[81]*Sappi che tosto...*: Italian for "Know that, as soon as a soul
betrays, as I did, its body is taken away by a demon... It throws
itself into such a cistern, to its ruin."

[82]*Ad infernum...*: Latin for "You shall be brought down to Sheol, to
the lowest depths of the Pit." (KJV.) Isaiah 14:11.

ing that in the ninth circle there was pride. Many things about it were unknown to me, and many reasonings were hidden; but in the Ice and nowhere else, under the Giants, in the depths of the lake, in the three mouths and near and around the first proud being, – I knew already that there were no other souls there than the proud.

XV.

So I knew how and where pride was punished in Dante's *Inferno*. Then I asked myself where and how was envy? Because immediately my thought jumped from that to this; not only because in the order of capital sins pride is first and envy second, but also because I found that the first was considered the mother of the second. In fact, St. Augustine said (*De Virg.*, XXXI) that pride gives birth to envy and never is it without such companion, and that the bad Angel (*City of God*, XIV 11) was proud and, for that reason, envious. Which Aquinas had learnt from Augustine, as did Dante, who affirmed (*Inf.*, I 111 and *Par.*, IX 129) that the envy of the first proud one was the reason for all humanity's evils. From which I inferred that pride was against God, envy against man. All the more so given that Dante himself declared, in the *Convivio* (I 4), that parity among the depraved is a reason for envy; because envy, according to him, could not have arisen in Man against God, only in men against men. Nor is that contradicted by the fact that the Angel was moved by envy against Man: because the former,

---

[83]*Aderire immobilmente...*: Latin for "to adhere to the evil that he desired, without moving."

similar in part and dissimilar in part to the latter, en-
vied the part that was in him most similar first: in his
happiness; and he wanted that the other not be dissimilar to him after the fact: in misfortune. So Lucifer
had envy of Adam and led him to the sin of pride: the
first proud one among the Angels caused the first
proud one among men. And as the Angel was proud,
and for that reason envious, so too Man from pride
passed to envy, and Cain's sin followed that of
Adam's. Cain was truly envious, and that Dante believed it, as does everyone else, the voice attests
(*Purg.*, XIV 133) "*Anciderammi qualunque m'apprende*,"[84] which resounded in the second band of
Purgatory. And in this way I was confirmed in my
thinking that envy differs from pride in this, that the
one is against men or, to say it better, against one's
Neighbor, and the other is against God; because it
seemed clear to me that as long as it was only the Angel and God there could not be the sin of pride, and
when the Angel had a Neighbor who was Adam, then
the sin of envy appeared; and similarly when Man, or
the human couple, was alone before God, he could
only be proud, but when he had a Neighbor, a brother
that is, then he was also envious. Soon a fact appeared
to nullify my reasoning but which strengthened it instead and made it certain: the fact that the extreme
ring of Ice is named after Cain, in which Ice I had
seen the punishment of pride. It is because Dante,
who considers the harm done to one's parents and
kinsmen an act done directly against God, making the
same Cain envious on the one hand, proud on the other, – Dante makes it clear that envy as such is ex-

---

[84]*Anciderammi*...: Latin for "Whoever catches me will kill me."

pressed in the latitude of human society, or against one's Neighbor, when what was expressed within the limited ambit of the first family was against God, but only because the very first Neighbor to be envious of was none other than his brother. And from this it follows that the less serious mode of pride is a more serious kind of envy, and that the one is closely related to the other. Whereupon I began to suspect that in Malebolge,[85] at the center of which gapes the well of pride, envy was punished, which Dante made Virgil call the fraud in which no trust is placed, the which fraud is merely a means of killing the natural bond of love, or the bond that binds men to each other. And all of a sudden, to prove it to myself, I remembered the passage in Purgatory where (XIII 37 ff.) love or charity is considered a virtue contrary to envy, as is manifest to everyone. To kill the bond of love or act in a way contrary to charity is therefore both an act of fraud by him who is not trusted, and of envy. Whence it seemed more probable to me that the aforementioned fraud and envy were the same offense. Indeed, even such Fraud is only fraud with respect to men, as with envy, because only God and those who continue to take after God are the object of the additional love that the simple defrauder does not forget. The which defrauder, in our manner of thinking, would be the only true deceiver because he has need of tricks, traps, concealed methods to overcome the person who, because he does not trust, keeps his guard up. Now, it is clear just how much these operations of the defrauder are also those of the envious; so that the wicked Beast that is on guard in the eighth circle no

---

[85]Malebolge: the eighth circle of Hell.

longer seems the dirty image of fraud and envy. Indeed, if envy is substituted for fraud, everything will
appear clearer in that symbol, and better understood
would be the voice of the duke:

> *Ecco la fiera con la coda aguzza*
> *Che passa i monti e rompe mura ed armi,*
> *Ecco colei che tutto il mondo appuzza.*[86]

Words that ring with their particular sound
only to him who understands that this serpent... with
the face of a just man is infernal envy itself, as St.
Augustine says: *it is the face... which*, as an ancient
said, *was sent from the bottom of Hell by Lucifer,
which he first used to deceive our first parents*.

XVI.

Yes: Geryon is the epitome of infernal envy, which
was the cause of all the evils done to humankind: the
more I looked for it in the valleys of Malebolge, the
more I became convinced. Already the first of these
sought those who with signs and ornate words renewed, together with Eve, the Biblical serpent's deceit; and the second, those who, like that serpent, always had a tongue quick with flattery: those two, in
summary, the one and the other, who in doing evil to
their Neighbor employed the same arts as the first
Tempter. In the third pit I saw simoniacs; and it goes
without saying how I became perplexed at first trying

---

[86]*Ecco la fiera*...: Italian for "Look at the proud one with the
pointed tail who passes over the mountains and crushes walls
and armies! Look at him who corrupts all the world!" *Inferno*,
XVII 1 ff.

to believe them invidious, those who adulterate the
things of God for gold and silver. In whom there is, I
said, avarice, impiety, or, for all I know, anything but
envy. But Dante himself reassured me on the true nature of the sin of simony:

> ... *la vostra avarizia il mondo attrista*
> *Calcando i buoni e sollevando i pravi.*[87]

It saddens the world; that is, it harms humanity, whom you wish evil upon, whose good you envy,
like Satan already; pushing down the good, doing
what envy does in short, which, as we often see, believes itself capable of causing no greater harm to the
good and the brave than by exalting the wicked and
inept. It has to do with, I added, while reading in Augustine (*City of God*, XV, 5), that diabolical *inviden-
tia,* whereby wicked people envy the good for no other reason than that they are good and others wicked.
Also, the sin of simony I concluded to be envy then,
and the avarice of merchants of divine things was intended to be something other than giving or receiving
of harm in the fourth lake. Nor did the other sinners in
Malebolge seem to me at odds with the general concept of envy, which is to look askance at the good of
one's Neighbor, or with the signification of the first
sin of envy, committed by Lucifer for the misfortune
of mankind: nor diviners who see nothing else in
front of themselves but Satan when he said, "You will
be Gods"; nor those who took on other forms, like Satan who turned himself into a serpent; nor the false

---

[87]*La vostra avarizia...:* Italian for "Your avarice saddens the world,
pushing down the good and lifting up the depraved." *Inferno*, XIX,
104-5.

who possess the principal vice of the devil who is a liar and the father of lies; nor the disseminators of scandal and schism who imitate the Enemy who was the author of the separation of men from God; nor the sad hypocrites (in particular addition, this, to the invidious) who under fine guises, with a benign look on their faces, practiced evil; the hypocrites who, as St. Gregory says (*Moralibus*, VIII 34), "*laudari de iustitia inchoata appetunt, praeesse ceteris etiam melioribus concupiscunt*";[88] nor the robbers who shapeshift into serpents, nor the barrators, nor the wicked counsellors. And other clues were not missing, placed here and there in order to warn the reader that Malebolge is the realm of envy. Pope Nicholas [III] writhes his feet when he learns that it is not Boniface who, he thought, with so much joy, had come to Hell before his time: "*Sei tu già costì ritto, sei tu già costì ritto?*"[89] And in this way all these damned souls are obsessed with envy: two jovial friars:

> *Quando fur giunti, assai con l'occhio bieco*
> *Mi rimiraron senza far parola:*
> *Poi si volsero in sè e dicean seco:*

> *"Costui par vivo all'atto della gola;*
> *E s'ei son morti, per qual privilegio*
> *Vannot scoperti della grave stola?"*[90]

---

[88] *Laudari de inchoata*...: Latin for "strive to be praised by inchoate justice, and long even more to lord it over others."

[89] *Sei tu già*...: Italian for "Is that you standing there? Is that you standing there?"

[90] *Quando fur giunti*...: Italian for: "When they arrived, they stood looking at me askance without saying a word, then they turned to

and Maestro Adamo:

> *O voi, che senza alcuna pena siete,*
> *E non so io perchè...*[91]

The damned appear to suffer because others don't suffer enough, so that a large part of their torment is due to their companions in suffering, like Caiaphas who must feel "*Qualunque passa com'ei pesa pria.*"[92] And so with the robbers, one changes, and the other transforms: "*io vo' che Buoso corra, com'ho fatt'io, carpon per questo calle*";[93] so too with the two shades, pale and naked, snapping at each other like pigs; and, similarly, Maestro Adamo and Sinone brawl, each one delighting in the greater punishment and more grievous sin of the other. Two devils brawl even, Alichino and Calcabrina, the latter of whom was desirous "*che quei compasse (ossia che succedesse un male, un disordine) per aver la zuffa*"[94]: the which desire is practically the principal character-

_____

each other and said: by the action of his throat this one looks to be alive, but if they are both dead, by what privilege do they go about without wearing the stole?" *Inferno*, XXIII 85 ff.

[91]*O voi, che...*: Italian for "O you who are without any punishment, and I do not know why..." *Inferno*, XXX 58 ff.

[92]*Qualunque passa...*: Italian for "the weight of whoever passes over [him]." *Inferno*, XXIII 120.

[93]*Io vo' che...*: Italian for "I want Buoso to run, as I did, down this road, on all fours." *Inferno* XXV, 140-141 ff.

[94]*Che quei compasse...*: Italian for "that the other should free himself (or that some bad thing should happen, a brawl) and have a quarrel." *Inferno* XXII, 133-135.

istic of envy. And to top it all nearly, to Dante, who weeps on seeing the tears of the diviners, Virgil says, rebuking him:

> *...ancor se' tu degli altri sciocchi?*
> *Qui vive la pietà quando è ben morta.*[95]

Which words, more than to the damned in general, refer in particular to those who act against charity, i.e., the envious, for whom not to have charity is to show homage to the charity that they offended.

XVII.

Then I considered the real reason for the "*Loco in inferno detto Malebolge*";[96] and its being made of stone and having a color of iron reminded me of the river bank and the path along the second ledge of Purgatory, which were shown to be "*Col livido color della petraia.*"[97] This similarity was not by chance, and the explanatory notes of the ancient critic, previously mentioned, helped me, which said about the simoniacs that *They are thick in the livid rock; that is, in the hateful hardness which they have for their neighbor, for whom they have no charity.*[98] And in another place: *In the world they were hard and obstinate like*

---

[95]*Ancor se' tu...*: Italian for "and are you as foolish as the rest of them? Here pity lives only when it is quite dead." *Inferno*, XX ff.

[96]*Loco in inferno...*: Italian for "place in Hell called Malebolge."

[97]*Col livido...*: Italian for "with the livid color of rock."

[98]*Sono fitti nella pietra…*: Commentary on the *Divine Comedy*, Francesco da Buti, (AD 1324-1406), the "ancient critic."

rocks and cold to any charity.[99] These correspondences moreover among the envious of Purgatory and
the fraudulent of Hell compelled me to seek out in
that Purgatory a confirmation for what I had concluded on pride, and intelligence for what I was about to
conclude on envy: confirmation and intelligence that
had to come to me from that Thomistic argument of
Purgatory, which had already established that it
would have to complete the Aristotelian explanation
given in the Hell. I saw in fact that there was an evident relationship between the malice that hate ac-
quires in heaven and the evil that is loved; since the
act of malice that is seen in Hell must have been pre-
ceded by that love of evil which is atoned for in Purgatory. But I still saw "*Che il mal che s'ama è del
Prossimo,*"[100] not for one's own self, not for the first
Being; and that made a great difference between the
malice of Hell and the triform love of Purgatory, so
that I could doubt that between pride and envy, which
are declared in that Purgatory (XVII 115-120), and
betrayal and fraud which are in Hell – that there was
an equality which had to exist there, if what I had
thought was true, – that betrayal was pride and fraud
envy. But my doubt was cleared up immediately on
considering that Aquinas (2nd of the 2nd, XXXIV 1)
disputes not only that God can be held in hatred by
some, not for Himself however, not for certain effects
of His that can in no way be contrary to human will,
but for certain other effects that repugn an inordinate
will, "*sicut inflictio poenae et etiam cohibitio pecca-*

---

[99]ibid.

[100]*Che il mal...*: Italian for "that the evil that is loved is for one's
Neighbor." *Purgatory* XVII, 113.

torum per legem divinam, quae repugnant voluntati depravatae per peccatum."[101] It was clear to me then, without the need for subtler inquiries and broader research, that in Purgatory where one loves the pain inflicted by God and one praises his law, there can be no sin in which hatred of God has any part, and that therefore in the definition made in it of the capital sins one must expect a difference from what is made of the same capital sins in Hell, because in the latter there is hatred of God, and in the former either there was none, or it was removed. And I found the same for hatred of oneself, because Aquinas says (1st of the 2nd, XXIX 4) that anyone *per accidens* can hate himself, "it occurring that certain people think they are for the most part that which they are in their corporal and sensorial nature; whereby they love themselves according to what they estimate themselves to be, but hate what they truly are, while wanting things contrary to reason." Also, this love of oneself which is really hatred, I said that it cannot be found in sins that are wept for on the seven ledges. With this thought in mind I read the definition of the proud:

> *É chi, per esser suo vicin soppresso,*
> *Spera eccellenza; e sol per questo brama*
> *Ch'el sia di sua grandezza in basso messo;*[102]

---

[101] *Sicut inflictio...*: Latin for "such as the infliction of punishment; and the prohibition of sin by divine law,... which repugns a will debased by sin." *Summa*, 2nd of the 2nd, XXXIV, 1.

[102] *È chi, per esser...*: Italian for "there are some who, by suppression of their neighbor, hope to excel, and for this reason they desire that he be abased to make themselves seem greater." *Purgatory*, XVII 115 ff.

I saw that this in no way contradicted the idea that Dante had, in Hell, formed of pride, as I had previously concluded that it had. In fact, in Purgatory a hope and a desire were punished; such that if the sinner had wanted to obtain what he hoped for, excellence, he would have needed to see his neighbor suppressed more and more over time until the latter was unable to be found before God himself, and whom he had to put down if he truly wanted to be first. But he only desired the abasement of his neighbor; so that if he had passed from desire to the deed, he would have realized that it was appropriate for him to hate, not his Neighbor, but God, who prohibited by his law and repressed by his punishment the fulfillment of that which he desired. And in what way was the invidious person different from the proud person? I read this too:

> È chi podere, grazia, onore, e fama
> Teme di perder per ch'altri sormonti,
> Onde s'attrista sì che il contrario ama.[103]

The proud man hopes, the envious man fears: the one hopes for what he could not possess if he did not put himself above God; the other fears losing what he has or thinks he has: the one would like to be the greatest, the other would be content remaining what he is; but both, in order to fulfill his hope or stop his fear, have the same desire: that one desires and this one wants that someone else go down. The proud

---

[103] È chi podere...: Italian for "there are some who fear to lose power, grace, honor, fame because another person rises above them, hence they grow sad to the point of loving the opposite." ibid, 118 ff.

man and the envious man do not differ then in their
desire for evil, and they would not differ in the sub-
stance of their wicked act; so that in the end, there is
the unrecognized excellence of the one, the which
would end in his opposing God himself; and the power and other human possessions of the other, for
which he finds himself alone, in contrast with other
men. And the envious man fears to lose and grows
sad, and for that reason he would be cautious and secret when stooping to the deed, and he would resort to
deceit, and he would be fraudulent; while the proud
man, he too proceeding to the deed, could take concealed ways to arrive at his end, but he would not be
less fraudulent by resorting to them himself because
his goal ought to be to suppress him who is legiti-
mately superior to himself by the advantage given to
him. By the definitions of Purgatory it was confirmed
then what I had concluded about pride, and highlight-
ed what I was about to conclude about envy in Hell:
that pride was punished, under the name of betrayal
or fraud (fraud of those in whom a trust is placed), in
the Ice; and envy, under the name of fraud (fraud of
those in whom no trust is placed), in Malebolge; and
that if the one is against the two parts of *Iustitia*,
called *Religio* and *Pietas*, the other is against the
Iustitia communiter dicta. In truth, this is among
equals, given that the envy that offends it can only be
among equals.

XVIII.

As envy with pride, so the sinners of Malebolge have
something in common with those of the Ice: the re-

pugnance of telling their name and of being known. Venedico believed he was hiding himself by lowering his face; Alessio Interminei screamed at Dante; Pope Nicholas sighs and speaks with a tearful voice; the diviners are all pointed out by Virgil; Ciampolo does not give his name, same deal for the other offenders, the Friars Gomita and Michel Zanche; Francesco de' Cavalcanti and Puccio Sciancato run off quietly; nor does Ulysses have any need to reveal himself, and Guido di Montefeltro responds without fear of infamy because he believes that Dante will never be able to return to the world, and Muhammad gives him his name because he believes him to be a soul that "*in su lo scoglio muse forse per indugiar d'ire alla pena*."[104] It is true that, as with traitors, so too with the fraudulent, some of them reveal themselves by their own initiative, but for some subtle, special reason whereby the general act and the reason for it is not infringed. The hypocritical Jovial Friars give their name because, even though being in Hell, they seem to hope to hide their guilt, as they did in the world; the disseminators of scandal and schism seem to overcome the horror of giving themselves away in the hope of planting yet new schisms and scandals, like those who reveal, in the act of revealing themselves, the names of other sinners; or, more simply, with the strong desire to inflict harm on their neighbor, which desire still lives in them, as is seen especially among the forgers. In any case, I observed that while the majority of fraudulent people were not desirous of fame, it was just the opposite with Bocca; and this I thought

---

[104]*In su lo scoglio*...: Italian for "on this cliff muses perhaps to delay going to punishment." *Inferno*, XXVIII 43-44.

was because, as pride is the love of one's own excellence, so envy is practiced "*rispetto a quei beni in cui è vanagloria e in cui gli uomini amano d'essere onorati e aver riputazione*"[105] (2nd of the 2nd, XXXVI). Which Virgil said in his definition:

> *È chi podere, grazia onore e fama*
> *Teme di perder...*[106]

And that was confirmed by the ancient one, whose words I have mentioned thrice; who, with respect to the sin of diviners and charmers, all pointed out by Virgil and not one among them having revealed himself, says that it *is contained under fraud insofar as sinners such as these are intent on vainglory and on making themselves honored and known...* So, therefore, I saw envy and pride similar even in this, in the love for fame, which the one group fears to lose and the other desires in a high degree, whence they were punished in Dante's *Inferno* with the vain desire for the opposite. But who presented himself to me, to confound all my reasonings, a sinner of the seventh pit who, instead of hiding himself and lowering his gaze and running off quietly, proclaimed: "I am Vanni Fucci, beast!" But all of a sudden I saw that Vanni Fucci lied and passed himself off for what he was not, so that by revealing himself to be a liar he furnished the confirmation of my observation. If he had really been who he said he was, and as Dante had

---

[105]*Rispetto a quei...*: Italian for "with respect to those possessions in which there is vainglory and in which men love to be honored and to have reputation."

[106]Original footnote: ibid, 118 ff.

seen him, a man of blood and violence, he would not
have been "placed so low." He who bragged of his
bestial life and of his being evil, when he believed he
could deceive Virgil, he depicted himself sad (the adjective of the invidious) with shame, when he could
not deny the guilt for which he was pushed further
down, which would not have suited his other misdeeds. There was then in this one wrong a shame that
was not contained in the others. Now, this shame re-
sulted of course from his not only being a man of
blood and violence, but also a thief, or rather to put it
more generally, a fraud. And Dante himself says that
fraud displeases God most: because fraud is man's
particular evil; which is almost a correction in part
and in part a declaration of what Tullius said (*De Off.*,
I 13,41): "*utrumque homine alienissimum, sed fraus
odio digna maiore.*"[107] Reason then, in this way, as it
distinguishes men from beasts, renders more serious
the harm that results from deceit; whence it is punished with more pain and shame. Whereof I was driv-
en – because I knew one element, the intellect, contained in fraud, or rather in envy and pride, – to seek
out others, in order to see whether I had erred perhaps
in believing as I believed. Looking into this, I came to
a point in the *Comedy* where the Angel of Hell is depicted in the very act of committing evil; and I read[108]

> *Giunse quel mal voler, che pur mal chied*
> *Con l'intelletto, e mosse il fummo e il vento*

---

[107]*Utrumque*...: Latin for "of the two most alien to man, fraud is
the most hateful."

[108]Original footnote: *Purgatory*, V 112 ff.

Per la virtù che sua nature diede;[109]

in which verses, however interpreted, I recognized attributes of the Angel of Hell: will, turned solely to evil, intellect, and the virtue that his nature gave. This natural virtue, which was somewhat obscure to me, was made clearer to me by another passage in the poem where the Nature of creating even elephants and whales was praised, but no longer Giants:[110]

> *Chè dove l'argomento della mente*
> *S'aggiunge al mal volere ed all possa,*
> *Nessuno riparo vi può far la gente.*[111]

Here is the intellect or mind and ill intent, as in the passage from Purgatory; and through the virtue that its nature gave, it is strength. Which in Giants is an attribute of their large body: and in the Angel of Hell it cannot be an attribute of the body, given it has no body, itself being of a totally intellectual nature. But to Angels, as well as to Demons, passions are attributed and tendencies that would suppose in them a sensory part of the soul, which it cannot have because it is incorporeal. On the subject of which, I was reading in the *Summa* (1st, LIX 4) that Dionysius says that in demons there is an "*furor irrationabilis et concu-*

---

[109]*Giunse quel mal voler...*: Italian for "He joined malice, which wants to practice evil, to his intellect, and moved the mist and wind by virtue of his nature."

[110]Original footnote: *Inferno*, XXXI 55 ff.

[111]*Ché dove l'argomento...*: Italian for "for where reason's argument is added to malice and strength, no rampart can be made against it."

piscentia amens,"[112] from which it is deduced that there is in them irascibility and concupiscence which, if located in the sensory part of the soul, cannot be found in either Demons or Angels, which do not have this sensory part. Now, Thomas responded: *"quod furor et concupiscentia metaphorice dicuntur esse in daemonibus"*;[113] and it appeared to me that the Poet had followed Dionysius in his affirmation and Thomas in his explanation, and that he had attributed, even if metaphorically, a natural virtue to the Angel of Hell in order to succeed in doing what the Giants did with strength, desire being ultimately sensorial, which is divided into concupiscence and irascibility (*Summa*, 1st, LIX 4 and elsewhere), and that it is *"proximus motui corporis nostri"*[114] (ib., XXI). To the devils, then, Dante attributed, along with the intellect and the will, sensorial desire. Now, the object of the first is truth, the second good, the third sensory good: whence in the Angel of Hell, on the contrary, the object of the intellect will be falsehood, the will evil, sensorial desire sensory evil. Which, just how much that agrees with the influence of the devil in Buonconte's action,[115] everyone may see for himself.

[112]*Furor irrationabilis...*: Latin for "irrational fury and insane concupiscence."

[113]*Quod furor...*: Latin for "because fury and concupiscence are said to exist metaphorically in demons."

[114]*Proximus motui...*: Latin for "most particular to the movement of our body."

[115]Buonconte: Guido di Montefeltro (AD 1250-1289), mentioned earlier. He was a Ghibelline who died in the battle of Campaldino against the Florentine Guelphs. He had given treacherous council to Pope Boniface VIII, which earned him a place in Hell.

XIX.

But this triple composition of the act of wickedness makes me think of the emperor of the dolorous kingdom, who has three faces on his head: one in the middle, vermillion; one to the right, somewhere between white and yellow; one to the left, black. And I immediately saw that the vermillion face was the will, whose object is evil; the black face, the intellect, whose object is falsehood; and somewhere between white and yellow, the metaphorical desire of the senses which has sensory evil as an object and which is divided into irascibility and concupiscence, as is indicated by the two colors in that face; and which can be called power, as much to say the possibility of doing evil, which the intellect suggests and the will commands. Now, given that in *"benigna volontade... si liqua (Par.* XV 1) s*empre l'amor che drittamente spira, come cupidità fa nell'iniqua,"*[116] so that I saw perverse love or the love of evil or cupidity correspond with ill intent, it appeared clear to me how Lucifer's three faces symbolized the Trinity of evil, the vermillion face being the iniquitous will wherein love, which does not directly inspire, clarifies, as opposed to the first love; and the white and yellow face, which signifies diabolical power, being contrary to divine power; while the black face, which expresses the argument of the mind, which is in demons, being at the height of understanding. Whereby I had a confirmation of the positioning of the three heads, in that I doubted from the beginning that the face placed in the

---

[116]*Benigna volontade*...: Italian for "benign will... love, which directly inspires, always clarifies, like cupidity in iniquity."

middle was contrary to love, to the Holy Spirit that is, which proceeds from the Father and from the Son, and that for this reason I believed it should have been placed last, as it is written on the gate of Hell; I read in Thomas (1st, XXXVII 1) that the Holy Spirit *secundum originem*[117] is the third person, but, *prout est amor*,[118] it is the middle connection between the two, Father and Son. So that Dante on the Gate of Hell had counted the three persons *secundum originem*, and in the three faces of Lucifer he had arranged them according to the Father's *habitude of love* for the Son. There was then Lucifer the Anti-God, unary and trinary, and at the same time there was the three-headed sin, constant in malevolence, intelligence, and power; pride was the origin of every sin, and pride was a special sin. And the six large wings, which extended two under each face, it appeared to me that they had to be the other six sins, but why they were arranged two by two I did not know; and the three winds, I suspected naturally what they were, but I did not dare to affirm. I saw of course not only why Judas was in the mouth of malevolence or hatred, and why Brutus, the philosopher, was in that of intellect, but also why Cassius was in that of power and sensorial desire and why he was said to be so strong-limbed, a sort of Giant. But I was interested in proceeding to examine the three-bodied Geryon, whom I believed to be a symbol of envy in the same way as the three-headed Lucifer was the symbol of pride. Geryon in fact appeared to be a mixture of three natures, having the face of a

---

[117]*Secundum originem*: Latin for "with respect to origin." *Summa*, XXXVII 1.

[118]*Prout est amor*: Latin for "as love." ib.

Man, the trunk of a Serpent, and two hairy arms right up to the armpits. Now, as envy resembles pride, I was expecting to find in the said three natures the intellect, malevolence, and strength or sensorial desire. And because Dante said that fraud was man's particular evil, because without the intellect he cannot devote himself to it, in the face of a just man with which the aforementioned fraud could only come to fulfillment, not only because he was just, but because he was a man, I saw the intellect; and in the trunk of the serpent which was the first author of every evil, wickedness; and nothing was left except the branches which because they were two reminded me of the two-colored [white and yellow] face of Lucifer and the sensorial appetite that is divided into irascibility and concupiscence. And in what way did symbol differ from symbol? in the same way as sin from sin. Now, envy not differing from pride unless in this, that the former in order to cause injury always has need of deceit, whereas the latter has no need, Geryon has the face of a just and benign man on the outside, and the trunk of a serpent, and the back and the chest and the ribs portrayed as made up of knots and little wheels; and pride being then, through the person who offends, the supreme and total transgression of the law, Lucifer has the crest, as if to say the crown, of the emperor that he is.

XX.

And I turned toward Vanni Fucci, who more than any other sinner in Malebolge made me think of envy with that sinister vaticination, who does it only so that

Dante might suffer pain. In fact, even after Dante becomes aggrieved, what does that suffering do for the
thief? In this way, envy wears itself out in vain labor;
such that the abasement of others will never diminish
its fear of losing what it possesses of power, favor,
honor, fame. But Vanni Fucci is ashamed of being
stuck in the misery where Dante sees him, he who
professes a bestial pride and to have loved a bestial
and not a human life. And not even Dante would have
thought he'd see him placed so far below, because the
sin that Vanni discounts was already attributed falsely
to someone else, and Dante sees him as a man of
blood and violence, i.e., as the ancient critic explained, a quarrelsome and murderous man. Now,
where would Dante have expected to find such a sinner? Where the sinner would have wanted to make
believe he merited being put: where one sees "*morte
per forza e le ferute dogliose che nel prossimo si dan-
no*,"[119] in "*La riviera del sangue, in la qual bolle qual
che per violenza in altrui noccia*."[120] Which Dante not
only clearly alluded to, saying that he had seen a man
of blood and violence, but which Vanni himself more
clearly expressed, professing: "A bestial and inhuman
life pleased me." In fact, between the malice by force
and that by fraud, the former is punished less because
it is not an evil particular to man, as fraud is, force being more common among animals. Whereas the thief
who by his words and the tone of his voice would appear altogether different from a hypocrite and seems

---

[119]*Morte per forza*...: Italian for "death by murder and painful
wounds that are inflicted on one's neighbor."

[120]*La riviera del sangue*...: Italian for "The river of blood in which
boils those who harm others through violence."

more intent on increasing rather than diminishing his guilt, it actually turns out that he attenuates his malice with those same words, like someone who affirms not having put his mind to it: which he had not. However, when, even after having been discovered for what he is, he cries out: "*Togli, Dio, chè a te le squadro,*"[121] it is clear that the thief wants to continue his game of passing for someone that he is not, pretending that he merits a different punishment than someone who has felt God's Justice, but it is not clear whether he now pretends to merit a more serious or a less serious punishment and to being more violent or more proud, violent like Capaneus or proud like Lucifer; so that Dante himself, who with the Aristotelian distinction of dispositions shows that he does not find the distinction Christian anymore, adds:

> *Per tutti i cerchi dell'inferno oscuri*
> *Non vidi spirto in Dio tanto superbo,*
> *Non quel che cadde a Tebe giù da' muri.*[122]

And in truth Vanni Fucci is bitter, like Capaneus who is not softened by the rain of fire. But Capaneus remains spiteful and distorted, and the thief escapes without saying a word, when he is caught by snakes, symbols of fraud. Now, Capaneus is not really guilty of that pride that Virgil supposes in him, saying "*in ciò che non s'ammorza la tua superbia se'*

---

[121] *Togli, Dio...*: Italian for "Take that, God, right back at you!" Inferno, XXV 3.

[122] *Per tutti I cerchi...*: Italian for "Throughout the dark circles of hell, I have not seen so proud a spirit against God, not even he who fell from the walls of Thebes." *Inferno*, XXV 13 ff.

tu più punito,"[123] nor is Vanni Fucci that spirit who appears, to Dante, so proud against God; because pride is associated with the intellect and Capaneus is violent, and in violence the intellect has no place, and Vanni Fucci in turn succeeds with his blasphemy only to make himself similar to Capaneus and in confirming himself a beast, in other words in committing a bestial and inhuman sin. Now, what is that sin?

XXI.

So I went looking; and I confess that with astonishment I saw here that not all interpreters of the Sacred Poem found the aforementioned Aristotelian disposition [of] mad bestiality entirely one with the malice by force or violence. Nothing was more clear, to be honest. Vanni Fucci, known as violent, as a man of blood and violence, who as such would be expected to be found in the first ring of the first circle surrounded by the rocks of the high escarpment, has no problem professing himself an animal and to having led a bestial and inhuman life, but has to confess by necessity, because the place and the mode of punishment are not in accordance with what he professes, to having also committed an evil act particular to man and for this reason to be kept below: oh! how not to understand immediately that violence is senseless, that it is bestial in fact, and that mad bestiality and violence are one and the same thing? And all of a sudden came a centaur onto the scene, full of rage, as if to confirm and retell the thing. Bad in truth, *semi-ho-*

---

[123] *In ciò che...*: Italian for "in that your pride is not exhausted, you are all the more punished."

mo and *semifer* as Virgil calls him, he is not like other centaurs in the first ring of the first large circle, although it would have been the right place for him not only as a symbol but as a perpetrator, given that "*sotto il sasso di monte Aventino di sangue fece spesse volte laco*"[124]; but he was also fraudulent, that is, insofar as an animal, as someone who was half-man, half-beast, he committed an act of fraud which is an evil particular to man. Whence the centaur, in addition to the snakes he has on his back,

> *Sopra le spalle, dietro dalla coppa,*
> *Con l'ale aperte gli giacea un draco;*
> *E quello affoca qualunque s'intoppa.*[125]

But here I paused, first doubting and then changing my doubt little by little into profound and long admiration. Why this dragon that breathes fire on whomever it meets? I asked myself. And immediately I rephrased my question. Why are the centaurs symbols of violence? Not only because they all used to go hunting in the world, not only because Nessus took his revenge on himself, not only because Pholus was so full of anger, but also and more so because the Centaurs are half-man and half-beast or bestial, or really proud. Thus the infamy of Crete, which seems an even more general symbol than the centaurs, is the aforementioned beast and compared to a bull and called bestial anger. But there was another symbol in

---

[124]*Sotto il sasso*...: Italian for "Under the rock of Aventino Hill, many a time he made a pool of blood."

[125]*Sopra le spalle*...: Italian for "On his shoulders, behind his neck, with its wings outspread, lies a dragon; and it breathes fire on whomever it meets." *Inferno*, XXV 22.

this first large circle: the ugly Harpies. Now, the
Minotaur, Centaurs, Harpies all have a thing in common, which is different from the symbols of Geryon
and Lucifer in the second and third large circles.
What is it? Two natures, while Geryon has three, and
Lucifer has three faces. But if the three faces of Lucifer and the three natures of Geryon portrayed
malevolence, intellect, and power, the necessary elements or heads of the sin of pride and envy; the two
natures of the symbols of sin punished in the first
large circle, the sin in which intelligence has no place
because force is not, like fraud, the particular evil of
man, – the two natures represent power clearly, which
I called sensory appetite and malevolence. And as the
two natures of the Minotaur, the Centaurs, and the
Harpies represented the subjective elements of sin, it
was made clearer by the fact that, having been placed
in another circle for the fraudulent furor that he created, or for having added to his bestial or violent Malice a third element, the intellect, the centaur Cacus assumed a third body or third nature which was meant
to suggest a "dragon on the shoulders, behind the
neck, with wings outspread." Which to me seemed a
most suitable addition, considering the snakes of the
pit and, even more, the filthy image of fraud that had
a serpent's tail. Okay: but here I was thinking again
about the three-bodied Geryon and its serpentine nature which I had concluded signified malevolence,
while it appeared to me that the intellect was represented by the face of a just man; and here instead, in
Cacus, I had to admit that by the dragon was signified, not malevolence, but intellect. But in Dante's
creation of the symbol of violence, bestial sin signi-

fied, by necessity, bestial nature by excluding from the symbol the element that would have represented the intellect; however, having the sin, bestial albeit, of the two elements that remained, one human and not feral, because animals don't have a will but only humans do, the symbol was half-human and half-feral. So the part that in the Centaurs, the Harpies, and the Minotaur could have represented reason had already been used by the symbolizer for the will; so that when he wanted a Centaur with a brain, he was constrained to take, in order to symbolize it, the Serpent that elsewhere had symbolized malevolence. And yet, what admirable sagacity! He knew how to repair the defect as best he could, placing the serpent on Cacus such that it lay on his head and was in a certain manner the same head of a Centaur, while the serpent in Geryon was his trunk and tail. And that confirmed that the making of such a new head for the Centaur, which breathes fire on whoever comes into contact with it, was precisely similar in effect to the the tail of Geryon, the which sweeps over the mountains and destroys walls and armies. So Cacus was three-bodied as well as a result: while his brothers and the Minotaur and the Harpies were two-bodied, because two elements only make up the sin, which they are the symbols and guards and punishers of. And in this I was assisted by such a proof as to submerge any doubt in me. I read that the sin more serious than violence was, in addition to disparaging nature and its goodness,

... far forza nella deitade

Col cor negando e bestemmiando quella;[126]

where in the lowest ring, beyond Sodom and Cahors,
is placed those who, disparaging God, speak earnestly. I didn't know whether others had understood these
words that negate God and speak disparagingly of
God in earnest: I knew that they could not be understood except in one way: only earnestly, or rather
with *ΘΥΜΟΣ*, with irascibility, with the sensitive part
of the soul, without competition of the intellect. In
fact, Capaneus stolidly threatens God with an ill-hu-
mored vengeance, even while he shoots arrows at him
with all his strength; and he is precipitated into Hell
precisely by God's arrow! Whence Virgil's words.
And that the intellect was missing in the first ring,
Dante had mentioned it explicitly, calling cupidity
blind and anger insane, which was punished in a river
of blood. All that remained then was to know about
the second [ring], given that those of the first had
sinned without competition of intellect, like homicides, and those of the third, like Capaneus. But those
who deprive themselves of the world, or gamble and
squander their means and lament when they should be
cheerful are clearly crazy in the way they act, which
wasn't necessary for Dante to say other than recount-
ing what they had done. Now, what was this sin or
bad disposition, called maliciousness, which pursues
its goal only with violence, without competition of intellect, also called mad bestiality? I reread: the infamy
of Crete...

Quando vide noi, sè stesso morse,

---

[126]*Far forza...*: Italian for "to wage violence against the deity with
a negating heart and blaspheming it." *Inferno* XI, 46-47.

Sì come quei, cui l'ira dentro fiacca;[127]

lies in madness then; it is called bestial anger then;
blinding anger is what it is called, that which immolates in the river of blood; one of the centaurs, although from afar, all of a sudden threatens to draw his
bow, and Charon immediately guides a boat in the direction of Dante and Virgil, on seeing them; Pier della
Vigna declares that he was moved by a disdainful
temper and calls the soul ferocious that tears itself
away from the body by itself; still filled with rage is
Capaneus, who lies spiteful and whose vexations
"*sono al suo petto assai debiti fregi*."[128] And then the
sinners who speak, they speak disdainfully, so that
anger appears to have been their habit in life if they
conserved it in death: it is not only Pier della Vigna
who speaks disdainfully of court prostitutes, but he
who turned his houses into places of torture and punishment, and Ser Brunetto remembering the city of
Baptiste[129] and its ungrateful and malicious people,
and Iacopo Rusticucci, asking whether courtesy and
valor has not totally abandoned his city, and Scroveni
saying to Dante, "Or te ne va,"[130] and preaching ill
fortune to his neighbor Vitaliano. Their sin would be
anger then? Oh! what do Sodom and Cahors have to
do with with anger? Anger sometimes enters into vio-

---

[127]*Quando vide noi...*: Italian for "when he saw us, he bit himself,
like those whom an internal ire wears down." *Inferno* XII 14 ff.

[128]*Sono al suo...*: Italian for "are duly adorned on his chest."

[129]Baptiste: Baptiste Cambray a weaver from the beginning of the
13th century who invented the fabric of same name.

[130]*Or te ne va*: Italian for "now get out of here."

lence, of course, but violence is not anger. That is what I was thinking, but I hesitated, perplexed.

XXII.

In any case, I had to understand how the Poet, under the same concept of violence or malice by force, put together in the same group, in addition to homicides and marauders, in addition to suicides and spend-thrifts, – blasphemers, sodomites, and usurers. Of these last three categories in particular, I did not understand the how or why. For there really was a group that Dante entreated Virgil to explain to him. Dante did not understand how usurers offended divine goodness, and Virgil obligingly explained how usury despises nature (and God consequently) in itself and in art. Fine: but how is there violence in such offense or in such contempt? Because even Lucifer offended God in his goodness, but he was not violent, just proud; and all sinners offend him who are the aforementioned perpetrators of this or that sin, not necessarily involving violence. To compel money to make money, without other proper business: this was the response that I got for my doubts. But it appeared to me a kind of speaking in metaphor, as ingenious a caviling as you want, not worthy of Dante. And honestly how is there no intellect in such "compulsion"? On the contrary, it is abundant, and subtle; while in violence it would not have to be. It was necessary to wait for Virgil's own words in order to get at Dante's thought. To Dante's question, – in what way does usury offend divine goodness – Virgil responds that the usurer contemns nature and God because he is going in another direction than that assigned by God to men. It is fitting that a man derive his maintenance and his advancement from nature and from art. It is fitting because God wants it thus, and it is written in Genesis. Thus does he want it in his goodness, because whoever acts differently offends that. Now, in what way did God principally show his goodness to man? In creating him similar to himself, not only intelligent therefore, but hardworking. From the beginning, Genesis says, "*Posuit Deus hominem in Paradiso ut operaretur...*"[131] And Thomas (1st, CII 3) reports here the comment by Augustine which says that that labor "would not have been tiring, as it would be after sin, but enjoyable through the practice of natural virtue." But then the work and the fatigue, and in particular agriculture, was imposed by God on man "*in poenam peccati*"[132] (ib.) because God was irate, as ire and the like are attributed to God, according to the similarity of effect; now, given that punishment stems from anger, his punishment is metaphorically called anger. God then said to man: "*Vesceris pane tuo in sudore vultus tui.*"[133] But which of these two passages from Genesis should we bring to mind in order to understand Dante's thought? In the first is expressed an act of goodness by God, in the second an act of his justice: consequently, the first appears more opportune to us than the second. But beyond the good

---

[131]*Posuit Deus hominem*...: Latin for "And the Lord God put man in the garden so as to work." Genesis 2:15.

[132]*In poenam peccati*: Latin for "in punishment for his sin."

[133]*Vesceris pane tuo*...: Latin for "You shall eat your bread by the sweat of your brow." Genesis 3:19.

standing in relation to the just, as genus stands in relation to species, should we not believe that Dante considered the justice of God in His punishment of the
first man as more "*condecentia suae bonitatis*"[134] than
a "*retributio pro meritis*"[135]? By the first in fact he
spares, by the second he punishes the wicked (*Summa*, 1st, XXI 1). Now, Man, predestined already in
punishment to be sheltered from divine goodness by
"*Sì alto e sì magnifico processo*"[136] (*Par*., VII 109,
113) was certainly not punished "*pro meritis*," and
had therefore a pardon rather than a punishment and
received the proof of God's goodness more than that
of his justice. Augustine (*City of God*, XIV 21) has a
comment through the exhortation "*crescite et multiplicamini*"[137] which Dante could have appropriated to
himself through this other divine warning. He says
that such benediction of nuptials "*fu data avanti il
peccato, perchè si conoscesse che la procreazione dei
figli pertiene alla gloria del connubio, non alla pena
del peccato*."[138] And thus work, because given as the
object before sin, conserved after sin the mark of divine goodness on the one hand, and retained the mark

---

[134]*Condecentia suae*...: Latin for "out of the goodness of his
heart." *Summa*. 1st, XXI 1.

[135]*Retributio pro meritis*: Latin for "reward of merit." ibid.

[136]*Sì alto e*...: Italian for "so high and so magnificent a process."

[137]*Crescite et multiplicamini*: Latin for "be fruitful and multiply."
From Genesis, 1:28.

[138]*Fu data avanti*...: Italian for "was given before sin, because it
was known that the procreation of children belongs to the glory of
marriage, not to the punishment of sin." *City of God*, XIV, 21.

of justice on the other, just as the procreation of children was the sign of the first and parturition with suffering as that of the second. And I concluded that in Dante's thought the usurer, subtracting himself from his work, disobeyed a precept in which there was without a doubt the castigation of ancient sin, but which had been given even before it by divine goodness. Therefore, it offended goodness even by refusing to do what the justice of God had enjoined, not only because of what justice had enjoined, what goodness had destined, but because justice was, in the punishment, more a condescension of God's goodness than a retribution according to man's merit, and because justice is, in any case, contained in the goodness, as the species is in the genus. But meanwhile the usurer, while succeeding to offend divine goodness, was acting however directly against justice, because only Adam in earthly Paradise could have acted against goodness by refusing to work. But Adam's sons are no longer in Paradise, and work for them is no longer free from fatigue: so immediately they rebel against justice and only mediately offend goodness.

XXIII.

Here I asked: how can man rebel against Justice? How can he not recognize it? Justice exists in giving to each person "*suum ius*";[139] whoever deems "*iniuria*" to be "*ius*", and Injustice Justice, does not recognize it. The usurer consequently deems injury as just; and rebels. But I was reading (*Summa,* 1st of the 2nd, XLVII 1) that "*ira est appetitus nocendi alteri sub*

---

[139] *Suum ius*: Latin for "his right" or "his due."

ratione iusti vindicativi";[140] and so from Thomas and others I learnt that the irate person meanwhile seeks a vengeance (*vindictam*) insofar as it seems right to him; and a just vengeance is not wrecked except for what was unjustly done; and therefore what provokes to anger is always something by reason of an injustice (ib., 2); and that anger is "*libido ulciscendi*"[141] (*City of God*, XIV 15) and that, in so many words,

> ... *è chi per ingiuria per ch'adonti*
> *Sì che si fa della vendetta ghiotto,*
> *E tal convien che il male altrui impronti.*[142] [143]

as Dante defines it. And behold, I understood somewhat better how he of the fat and blue sow had been collocated under the stratum of fire in the same ring as him who said: *Primus in orbe deso fecit timor.*[144] For it appeared clear to me, now that I had made the connection between violence and anger, how men like Capaneus and Scrovegni could be called violent. Verily, the usurers appear offended, as if by insult, by the castigation justly given by God to men "*di nutrirsi*

---

[140]*Ira est appetitus...*: Latin for "Anger is the desire to harm another because of a just vindication."

[141]*Libido ulciscendi*: Latin for "desire for revenge."

[142]Original footnote: *Purg.*, XVII 121 ff.

[143]*È chi per ingiuria...*: Italian for "there is he whom injury appears to offend, making him greedy for revenge, so that he prepares to do another harm."

[144]*Primus in orbe...*: Latin for "fear made the first gods in the world." The phrase is spoken by Capeneus in the *Thebaid*, III 661. Publius Papinius Statius (AD 45-96).

del pane loro nel sudore del loro volto,"[145] and they become eager for vengeance. But how can it be a vengeance against God? In this regard, I knew quite well that the sinner sinning "can effectively nowise harm God, however for his own part he can act deceitfully against God; firstly, by contemning his commandments; second, by inflicting harm on someone, himself or another person: which is effectively against God, by the fact that he whom he harms is contained within God's providence and tutelage" (*Summa*, 1st of the 2nd, XLVII 1). Now, what is vengeance? Dante explained it to me in the last verse of the above-quoted tercet, a verse that I realized I did not fully understand: in which he mentions evil as something, as if to say some act or the like, received by him who needed to act immediately in kind to the person who did it to him. Now, it is opportune to consider that, according to Thomas, who follows Aristotle in this, all causes of anger can be reduced to "*parvipensio*" or "*despectio*," in other words contempt (1st of the 2nd, XLVII 2). So the usurer avenges himself on God by offering contempt for contempt, for he contemns nature for itself and for its followers, and consequently God; like Capaneus, who remains spiteful and had remained spiteful and because he held God in disdain. But how can the usurer believe himself contemned by God? "*Parvipensio*" or contempt, says Thomas (ib.), "is opposed to man's excellence; in that those things that men consider in no way, shape or form to be worthy, they contemn, as it is said in the second Rhetoric: now, from our posses-

---

[145]*Di nutrirsi del pane...*: Italian for "to nourish themselves on bread in the sweat of their brow."

sions we want some excellence: and for this, any harm brought to us, in as much as it derogates from excellence, appears to belong to contempt." Now let's think about the [usurer's] purse which has a certain color and a certain sign on it, on which the eyes of these sinners feed: we will see just how insightfully the Poet depicts in what way they were desirous for some excellence and for what reason they were inclined to be contemptuous of the commandment that makes man derive his nourishment from his [effort and] fatigue. Who can affirm to have understood anything of this strange mutual "nobility" of Dante's usurers? And he confirms it to himself that their sin is anger, because all the reasons for anger are reduced to *parvipensio*. They are located, then, up at the very beginning of that seventh circle, like the proud imitators of Cain neighboring on the envious; in order to show how their offense had something of fraud in it; for in their desire to avenge themselves on God "they bring harm... to others." But even acting directly against God, they are not placed further below, because their sin, which is not an evil particular to men, is without the competition of intellect and therefore cannot be anything but anger.

XXIV.

Violence is without the light of intellect; therefore, it is mad bestiality or anger that is "*furor brevis*";[146] bestiality is the appetite for vengeance; therefore, it is anger. Thus had I concluded, thus did I have to conclude. But anger contains reason, says Thomas. Okay;

---

[146] *Furor brevis*: Latin for "brief madness."

but he contends (1ˢᵗ of the 2ⁿᵈ, XLVI 4) that its reason
is *quodammodo,*[147] for reason does not accompany
anger unless it is as a denunciator of the insult to be
avenged; and anger "does not perfectly listen to it, because it does not observe the rule of reason when exe-
cuting its vengeance; so that some quantity of reason
is requisite for anger, and it acts as an impediment."
Now, I saw the Minotaur's sudden turn to anger correspond perfectly with this concept because, upon
seeing Dante and Virgil, "*sè stesso morse, Sì come
quel, cui l'ira dentro fiacca.*"[148] Why? Because he believed, as Virgil is reproving him, that the Duke of
Athens, his murderer,[149] was there with him. Which is
then an act of reason that manifests or recalls the ancient injury done to Crete's infamy; whence he grows
angry on seeing the two visitors in Hell, desiring
vengeance. But Virgil wants to render him harmless,
and that is why he arouses in him the thought of that
insult from the time he was still alive; whereupon the
man-bull changes and seems only a bull, and becomes
bestial: that is, the act of reason, which the insult contained in Virgil's words stirs him to, is followed by an
impediment to that reason: which allows Virgil and
Dante to run to the boat easily, while the man-bull is
blinded with fury. Thus did I see that reason naturally
reveals an injury, supposed or real, done to all violent
men, which they crave to avenge, but that in doing so
they forget their reason. Thus it appeared to me that

---

[147]*Quodammodo*: Latin for "of a certain manner."

[148]*Sè stesso...:* Italian for "he was bitten, like someone whose
anger gnaws at him from within." *Inferno*, XII 14-15.

[149]Duke of Athens: Theseus, who slayed the Minotaur.

Dante was thinking of tyrants, just how tyrants were precisely, because their justice had not been what it needed to be, which Dante indicates, speaking of Arrigo (*Epistle*. V 3): "*semper citra medium plectens.*"[150] About Arrigo he says that, like Caesar, he will pardon those who implore mercy, so that his majesty "*de fonte defluat pietatis*";[151] and like Augustus, "*relapsorum facinora vindicabit.*"[152] By the same token, sovereigns naturally must punish crimes, but have to castigate "*citra medium*" and have compassion: if not, they are tyrants. Now, of those in the river of blood, it is precisely the merciless who complain of the damages, or rather the punishment given without listening to compassion, which it is justice and reason to listen to. As for personal vengeance then, which Dante considers just (*Inf.*, XXIX 16 ff), he puts forward the example of Guido di Monforte who, being right to vindicate himself against Eduardo Re, was wrong *in rependendo vindictam*[153] for the person he avenged himself on, and for the place, in God's lap, and for the means by which he avenged himself. Nor are the destroyers and robbers punished in the seventh circle instead of the eighth for any other reason than their having learnt of an offense that, rightly or wrongly, they desired to avenge themselves of (the

---

[150]*Semper citra medium plectens*: Latin for "always punishing moderately [between justice and mercy]." *Epistle*, V 8.

[151]*De fonte defluat pietatis*: Latin for "derives from a fountain of compassion." ibid., V 7.

[152]*Relapsorum facinora vindicabit*: Latin for "he will avenge the crimes of those who have relapsed." ibid., V 10.

[153]*In rependendo vindictam*: Latin for "in exacting his vengeance."

which is still the opinion and habit of road warriors), but not having listened to reason in following through with the vindication itself, especially after having taken it out on everyone, without waiting long enough to see whether they were guilty or not: whence their blind cupidity. In no one did that appear more manifest than in Pier della Vigna: whom the Poet makes demonstrate and swear that he did not betray his lord and hence that he was wrongly accused and blinded or imprisoned, whence his just resentment for a real injury. But reason later abandoned him:

> *L'animo mio per disdegnoso gusto*
> *Credendo col morir fuggir disdegno*
> *Ingiusto fece me contra me giusto*:[154]

where "*l'animo mio*" is to be noted, which is precisely the word θυμός that Thomas uses (1st of the 2nd, XLVI 8), when he concludes: *nihil autem prohibet, ut* θυμός *graece, quod latine furor dicitur, utrumque importet, et velocitatem ad irascendum, et firmitatem propositi ad puniendum.*[155] Even Pier della Vigna then, abandoned of his reason, which rightly identified the injury and the calumniatress however, targeted the wrong person in his vengeance, punishing himself and not the other. Anger indeed is mad, it is

---

[154]*L'animo mio...*: Italian for "my mind, by disdainful temperament, thinking to escape disdain in death, made me unjust who was just." *Inferno*, XIII 70.

[155]*Nihil autem prohibit...*: Latin for "nothing however prohibits that θυμός, which in Latin means *furor*, should mean both quickness to anger and firmness of purpose to punish." *Summa*, 1st of the 2nd, ILVI 8.

crazy, it is a "*pazzia breve*";[156] an insanity that can, while it rages, be found in people who are normally very reasonable; whereby Dante under the protection of the Half-brute lets us see men like Pier della Vigna and others who put forward ingenious stratagems to do good, and whom Dante would have wanted to embrace, and before whom he could show reverence. But here I too exclaimed, like Dante, upon seeing one of such family: "Are you here, Ser Brunetto? The sin in which you soiled yourself, how can it be anger?" But then the book of Genesis came to my aid, and suddenly I understood, that just as the excellent and noble usurers were violent against Art and for that reason against Nature and therefore perpetrators of anger against God, so were these literate luminaries and those of great fame perpetrators of anger against God because guilty of violence against Nature. In fact, their sin is against nature, "*in quantum impeditur generatio prolis*"[157] (*Summa*, 2nd of the 2nd , CLIV 1). And in summary against God's blessed injunction: "Be fruitful, and multiply, and replenish the earth, and subdue it..." Which injunction, as it was given before the first parents had eaten the apple, attested to the sanctity of marriage and was a sign of divine goodness. But after the sin, the lugubrious words were pronounced; God said "unto the woman...: 'I will greatly multiply thy sorrow and thy conception: in sorrow thou shalt bring forth children; and thy desire shall be to thy husband, and he shall rule over thee.' And unto Adam he said: 'Because you hast

---

[156] *Pazzia breve*: Italian for "brief insanity."

[157] *In quantum impeditur...*: Latin for "insofar as it impedes the generation of children." *Summa*, 2nd of the 2nd, 154 1.

hearkened unto the voice of thy wife, and hast eaten of the tree, of which I commanded thee, saying, Thou shalt not eat of it: cursed is the ground for thy sake; in sorrow shalt thou eat of it all the days of thy life; thorns also and thistles shall it bring forth to thee; and thou shalt eat the herb of the field; in the sweat of thy face shalt thou eat bread, till thou return unto the ground; for out of it wast thou taken: for dust thou art, and unto dust shalt thou return.'"[158] Now, the invitation to the nuptials that exists even after this intimation of death and misfortune can make what was a blessing seem like a malediction, and make believe that the glory of marriage is a punishment of that sin: whence men rebel, in their anger, against the providence of God who "*masculum et feminam fecit eos*."[159] Why make infelicity "be fruitful"? Why "multiply" death? Because he did not want that through them a "generatio prolis"[160] followed, scorning both nature and consequently God, he wanted to avenge himself of their contempt for God, which those great literary men and men of great fame more than others felt in their heart. In this manner, I began to understand how the sin in which Ser Brunetto had soiled himself did not prevent Dante from holding his head down as a man showing reverence; and even how Dante could act before such a band who now and then taught him how a man becomes eternal on earth. And I remembered how in those days there were sects

---

[158]Unto the woman he said...: (KJV.) Genesis 3:16-19.

[159]*Masculum et feminam*...: Latin for "made them masculine and feminine." Mark 10:6.

[160]*Generatio prolis*: Latin for "generation of offspring."

or congregations that were reputed guilty of similar
rebellions against God, and that the Cathars, as Mone-
ta said, affirmed it as illegitimate, i.e., against God's
law, the joining together even in matrimony, "*quia
credunt corpus maris et foeminæ a diabolo fuisse fac-
tum*"[161] (Tocco, *Eresia*, p. 90, n. 1), and the Almari-
ciani, beginning with the principle that the distinction
of gender was due to sin, "*et stupra, come Martino
Polono asseriva, et adulteria in charitatis nomine
committebant*"[162] (ib., p. 413, n. 2); and I admired the
Poet who so loftily conceived of man's sin, depicting
it in that eternal first drama, within and without the
paradise they delight in, where the voice of God was
heard and the Cherub's sword flashed; which Dante
had warned his good reader about, recalling Genesis:
when I suffered what the first Angel suffered, the
feeling that his rise was his fall. I heard in fact on the
seventh ledge of Purgatory one of the two groups of
lechers shout out loudly, Sodom and Gomorrah. They
were clearly perpetrators of the sin of Ser Brunetto,
and their sin was clearly that of lust: therefore I had
erred and all my argument had been, on this point,
and perhaps in everything, in vain.

XXV.

Moreover I thought, as I had already seen, that one
had to expect a difference between Purgatory and

---

[161]*Quia credunt...*: Latin for "because they believe that the body of
a male and a female was made by the devil."

[162]*Et stupra...*: Latin, with some Italian, for "and they committed
rape, as Martino Polono asserted, and adultery in the name of
charity."

Hell, insofar as among the sins that are punished in Hell are hatred of God and hatred of oneself, which are not the sins one expects to see in Purgatory. Hence I hoped to find something better. How could someone in all honesty hope to make himself a beautiful soul, who hated what it truly was, and who wanted something contrary to reason? Indeed, how could someone hate God who unless he turned to God in a paroxysm of love would not climb the holy mountain? Manfred says:

> ... io mi rendei
> Piangendo a Quei che volentier perdona.
>
> Orribil furon li peccati miei,
> Ma la bontà infinita ha sì gran braccia,
> Che prende ciò che si rivolge a lei.[163] [164]

Without that cry of contrition, he merited perhaps the Ice; but he surrendered in time, although at the moment of death, to That from which he had distanced himself in life with his sins. And what they were, Dante does not say, and it is not known whether he believed in what many believed in: in any case, in every sin there is a distancing, or turning away, from God, there is an "*aversio*"; indeed, the sin that he commits is mortal and to be punished eternally, when one reaches the very end of one's distancing, from God that is (*Summa,* 1st of the 2nd , LXXII 5): now this

---

[163]Original footnote: *Purg.*, III 119 ff.

[164]*Io mi rendei...*: Italian for "I gave myself over, in tears, to Him who willingly pardons. My sins were horrible, but infinite goodness has so great an arm that it takes back whatever returns to it."

aversion is no longer certain in those who converts or turns back. Which is indicated in Thomas with these words: "When for grace the guilt is remitted, the distancing (*aversio*) of the soul from God is removed, insofar as through grace the soul joins God. Whence and by consequence the condemnation to eternal punishment is lifted" (3rd, LXXXVI 4). But he adds: "The condemnation to some punishment can remain temporary however." Now, how is that? Because in every sin there is not only the "*aversio ab incommutabili bono*,"[165] but also the "*inordinata conversio ad commutabile bonum*"[166] (1st of the 2nd, LXXXVII 4 *passim*). Dante says (*Purg.*, XVII 115 ff) what this commutable good is for pride, envy, anger: excellence is what pride hopes for; power, favor, honor, fame is what envy fears to lose; vengeance is what hotheads are greedy for. He then falls silent as to the other good that does not make men happy, which the greedy and prodigal, the gluttonous, and the lustful abandon themselves too much to; but it is easy enough to guess at. And I hesitated to resolve a doubt, which presented itself to me all of a sudden. Sins are divided by Theologians into spiritual and carnal. Carnal sins would be, according to Gregory, only lust and gluttony; but others, following Saint Paul (Ephesians, V) who names *avaritia* in addition to *fornicatio* and *immunditia,* add avarice; and of these Dante was certainly one: who, in something else (apart from his opinion on the angelic hierarchy; *Par.*, XXVII 132) appears not to be in agreement with Gregory, in that,

---

[165]*Aversio ab*...: Latin for "aversion from an incommutable good."

[166]*Inordinat conversio*...: Latin for "inordinate conversion to a commutable good."

by saying that carnal sins are *minoris culpae* but *infamiae maioris*,[167] Dante, as if correcting him, says of incontinence (*Inf.*, XI 84) that the less it offends God, the less blame he finds. So Dante puts avarice or, better yet, prodigality, among the carnal sins or those of incontinence, following Thomas who explains (*Summa,* 1st of the 2nd, LXXII 2) *Potest dici, quod res, in qua delectatur avarus, corporale quoddam est*[168]; and as the most serious of the three. But these three are even less serious than spiritual sins, which (*Summa*, 1st of the 2nd, LXXIII 5) "pertain to the spirit, of which turning toward God and distancing oneself from him is typical, while carnal sins are consumed in the delectation of carnal appetite which the attraction to corporal affection principally pertains to; and for this reason, carnal sin, as such, has more conversion, because it is also of greater adhesion; but spiritual sin has more aversion, from which proceeds the reason for guilt, and this is why spiritual sin as such has greater guilt." Now, this is where my doubt lies: given that in Purgatory the perpetrators of spiritual sins can no longer be in an estrangement from God, why are they not placed on the upper ledges? In truth, St. Thomas observed (2nd of the 2nd, CLXII 6) that "as far as conversion is concerned, pride does not have to be the greatest of sins: because eminence (*celsitudo*), which the proud man inordinately craves, does not have the greatest repugnance to the good of virtue, ac-

---

[167]*Minoris culpae... infamiae maioris*: Latin for "minor in offence... greater in infamy."

[168]*Potest dici...*: Latin for "it can be said that what the greedy delight in is a corporal thing."

cording to his reasoning."[169] And while in Purgatory Dante places pride as the greatest of sins, putting it on the lowest ledge, he also declares that it craves no other thing than excellence itself "which according to his reasoning does not have the greatest repugnance to the good of virtue." And with that the doubt is resolved; Dante says this in fact:

> *È chi per esser suo vicin soppresso*
> *Spera eccellenza;*[170]

And as with pride, so too with envy and anger, he affirmed that the result was evil against one's neighbor. So Dante had conceived these three sins, or at least pride, in a manner all his own; so that nobody should marvel at what had appeared to me: that he had punished pride and envy and anger in the same way as betrayal (or fraud by someone who is trusted), as fraud by someone who isn't trusted, and as violence or bestiality. And in this way I came to the point where I had lost the hope for eminence; to the point where I saw all my reasonings were in vain, realizing that Sodom, which I had believed for Dante was the sin of anger or violence or bestiality, which are one and the same thing, was instead, for him, as for everyone, the sin of lechery. Oh! I said, but the sodomites of Purgatory rendered themselves unto God, entered

---

[169]As far as conversion...: From the Latin: "*Ex parte autem conversionis, non habet superbia quod sit maximum peccatorum, quia celsitudo, quam superbus inordinate appetit, secundum suam rationem non habet maximam repugnantiam ad bonum virtutis.*"

[170]*È chi per esser...*: Italian for "there are those who hope for excellence by pushing someone else down."

into Purgatory after a just penance. Now, what good
did penance have on their offense? St. Thomas responded (3rd, 86 4): "By grace, the mind's aversion
from God is removed, together with the condemnation to eternal punishment: what is left however is
material, in other words the inordinate conversion to a
created good, by which he must be condemned to a
temporal punishment." Except however for what in
the sin of the sodomites was really more of a distancing from God, in other words, the will to prevent the
generation of offspring, the material act still remained, which is lust. And thus not only was I confirmed in my thinking, but I found a new strength that
inspired me to continue looking, with the certitude
that I would find. To be honest, I turned to other interpreters and asked them, why didn't you explain
why Dante hadn't placed Brunetto with the lechers in
Hell, given that he had put Guinizelli with them in
Purgatory; and I felt that they would not have been
unable to give or that they could not give a reason
why he was there. Instead, I could still remember
what Thomas affirmed, how one sin could be com-
posed of multiple deformities and, by way of example, repeat what he said about adultery, how it not
only belongs to the sin of lust but also to the sin of injustice (1st of the 2nd, LXXII 2).

XXVI.

So then I knew that the aversion from God was missing in the sins of Purgatory and that, of them, only the
conversion to a commutable good was to be punished.
Whereas, in those of Hell, aversion from God was

punished with eternal suffering. Purgatory was [com-posed] completely of men converted to God; Hell was of men averse to God. I found it significative that the Poet made it so that none of the sinners uttered the name of God; except Capaneus, the man violently against God, whom he mentioned disdainfully as *Jove* (*Inf.*, XIV 52), and Vanni Fucci, the fake violent man who with the obscene gesture yelled: *Togli, Dio*[171] (*Inf.*, XXV 3). So many times when a damned person wants to refer to God, he prevaricates or con-ceals; and so Francesca (V 91) says, "The King of the universe"; and Farinata, "the Big Boss" (X 102); and Ulysses, "someone else" (XXVI 141); and Maestro Adamo, "rigorous justice" (XXX 70); in the same way that Virgil, who even pronounces the name of God, hints at however and conceals the name of Christ, calling him "a Powerful person" (IX 53); "He who harrowed Hell" (XII 38), "the Man who was born and lived without sin" (XXXIV 115). And I omit, as is evident to everyone, that Hell itself was facing in the opposite direction to that in which one climbs to God and that, with respect to God, Lucifer and all his dolorous flock are upside down. Now, I noted that in every mortal sin there is aversion and conversion; but that carnal sin nevertheless has more conversion, and spiritual sin more aversion, and that it is for this reason more serious than the former (*Summa*, 1st of the 2nd, LXXIII 5). And this I knew to be the reason for which Dante had collocated carnal sins, which for him also included avarice, outside Dis and beyond the Styx. Incontinence offends God less, he said; it offends him nonetheless and by consequence

---

[171] *Togli, Dio*: Italian for "Take that, God!"

there is also eternal punishment. For, while in every
mortal sin there is aversion and conversion, in some
however the former is predominant, in others the latter; and the one involves the other (*S.*, 2nd of the 2nd,
XX 1). So that in the sin of lust, there is conversion to
carnal pleasure which brings with it the aversion from
God, and in the sin of pride there is instead the aversion from God which produces the conversion to
something of the earth. And the other carnal sins are
like lust, and the other spiritual ones like pride. And
pride, says St. Thomas (2nd of the 2nd, CLXII 6), "*excedit in aversione.*"[172] Which, – as he gives the exact
explanation of the order in which these six sins are
punished in Hell: lust, gluttony, avarice, which are
carnal; anger, envy, pride, which are spiritual; – illuminates us with new intelligence into Dante's profound conscience. Because we see how he punishes
among the lechers the adulterers Paolo and Francesca,
signifying with this that conversion in them had pre-
ceded aversion; that a love offense was theirs, love
that, rapt, seizes a gentle heart,[173] love that no loved
person is exempt from;[174] that in their incestuous
adultery there was no sin of injustice; that the murderer of his wife and brother, although they were guilty,
was more guilty than they were; and showing thus,
before fainting and falling,[175] compassion for the two

---

[172]*Excedit in aversione*: Latin for "exceeds in aversion."

[173]Love that, rapt,...: "*amor, ch'al cor gentil ratto s'apprende.*"
Inferno, V 100.

[174]Love that no loving person is exempt from: "*amor, ch'a nullo
amato amar perdona.*" *Inferno*, V 103.

[175]Fainting and falling: *Inferno*, V 141-2.

family members. And we see likewise in spiritual sins that the aversion from God through desire or absolute primacy, or power, honor, favor and fame, or vengeance, had to suggest to the intellect turned to evil an insult to God and to whoever still cares for God or to men; or on the other hand to passion, to the feelings, an insult to God, to oneself, to one's Neighbor; for this reason it was punished eternally. Thus, Dante did not place pride in Hell unless as betrayal, envy unless as fraud, anger unless as bestial violence done against one's neighbor, against oneself, against God, Nature, and Art.

XXVII.

But if anger is punished in the seventh circle, what are punished in the Styxian bog, "*L'anime di color cui vinse l'ira*"?[176] So I returned in my mind to the place and dark hour of the Inferno; to which the more I thought about it, interrupting my reasonings, the more I said to myself that I owed them my attention, even when they appeared to contradict the more apparent truth. Now, then, I looked at the matter again, where I had left off, and I asked myself who those souls were, and what their misdeeds. One thing was very clear, that those of the fertile bog, like the lechers, the jealous, the greedy, and the prodigal, had sinned through that disposition that the *Ethics* calls incontinence, in the same way that the felons of the eighth and ninth circle were guilty of malice, and those of the seventh of mad bestiality. And incontin-

---

[176]*L'anime di color...*: Italian for "the soul of those overcome by anger." *Inferno*, VII 116.

ence is, according to the same Dante (*Purg.*, XVII
136 ff), the abandonment of oneself through excessive love for a good, which is a good even if it does
not make the man happy; it is (ib., 97 ff) not to limit
oneself as the said love for terrestrial goods does, it is
one's paying more attention to a good than one
should. And he also defines in general the incontinent
in Hell, adumbrating even the lechers in specific (*Inf.*,
V 38 ff.): "*i peccator carnali, che la ragion som-
mettono al talento.*"[177] Now, what is lust? It is what
Dante still called *libito*;[178] it is sensory appetite; in
fact, that part of it which is called concupiscible. So
in carnal sinners reason no longer performs its office
of moving its will, which is between reason and lust
(*S.*, 2nd of the 2nd, CLV 3); but lets something else
move it according to its pleasure. And I asked myself,
along with many others: can incontinence be different
than lust? [Aristotle's] *Ethics* in truth (VII 4) distinguishes between the absolutely incontinent, in other
words those who are such with regards to the pleas-
ures of the body, and the incontinent with regards to
an attachment to this or that. And in the sixth section
he distinguishes between the incontinent of anger and
those of concupiscence, and he calls the former less
filthy than the latter; the former acting according to
reason to a certain degree, and the latter not. Then
there is something of an incontinence of concupiscence, likewise an incontinence of irascibility, parties,
both the one and the other, to sensory appetite; which
Thomas confirms in many places in the *Summa* (2nd of

---

[177]*I peccator carnali*...: Italian for "the carnal sinners, who subject
reason to their lust."

[178]*Libito*: Italian for "pleasure, desire."

the 2nd, LIII 6, CLVI 4, CLVIII 4, CLV 2, CLVI 2).
Fine and good: but how different is incontinence in
anger from being guilty of anger or violence or bestiality? And Dante even places those guilty of anger in
the seventh circle, inside Dis, affirming thereby that
they are not incontinent. So what are they then? They
are men who caused harm, as a consequence of the
incontinence of anger. Because for Dante anger is not
anger unless it has some evil as its end, as envy is not
envy, nor pride pride without harm done to someone
else. Now then, if we suppose that the incontinent of
irascibility are those of the fertile bog, whom anger
overcame, as we know that the incontinent of concupiscence belong to the three anterior circles, those
who submit reason to lust, we must infer that they did
not do harm, because otherwise they would have been
placed lower, in the seventh circle. So I was thinking;
and I saw that in the swamp were muddy people with
offended looks on their face, one of whom was
named, Filippo Argenti, who in the end turned on
himself with his teeth;[179] and no mention of whose
crime was made, and only this was said about him:
"*Bontà non è che sua memoria fregi.*"[180] And I concluded that it could very well be that that bizarre char-
acter and the other naked people had been incontinent
in anger, but that they had not done any evil to others,
even if they had wanted to, continually gnawing away
at themselves with hatred and fury: which was signified by the evil that they were, by divine justice, con-

---

[179]Filippo Argenti...: "'*Filippo Argenti!*' e 'l fiorentino spirito in sé
medesmo si volvea co' denti." *Inferno*, VIII 63.

[180]*Bontà non è*...: Italian for "There is no memory of him having
done any good." *Inferno*, VIII 47.

strained to cause themselves there below, "*Trocandosi coi denti a brano a brano*,"[181] and turning on
themselves, as one of them does, with his teeth. And
suddenly all the naked people reminded me of other
wicked people, also naked (*Inf.*, III 64 ff.), they also
continually in motion, they also continually tormented, although by big insects and wasps and not by
companions in torture or by themselves. There were
many other similarities: Virgil chattered about it to
Dante, saying, "Let's not think about them, but look
and move on"; at this moment Virgil clasps Dante by
the neck and kisses him and calls him, "*Alma sdegnosa*,"[182] because he had driven Argenti away; here
and there he recognizes a Shade, and he does not
speak the name of the first one, and he does not name
the second, common souls; "*Fama di loro il mondo
esser non lassa*,"[183] Virgil says of the wicked; "*Bontà
non è che sua memoria fregi*,"[184] he says of Filippo
Argenti. Bad was the heart of angels that were in it
for themselves, bad souls and all that sect; goodness
does not adorn the memory of arrogant people. And
this one exclaims: "*Vedi che son un che piango*";[185]

---

[181] *Trocandosi coi denti*...: Italian for "gnawing away at themselves
piece by piece." *Inferno*, VII 114.

[182] *Alma sdegnosa*: Italian for "indignant soul." *Inferno*, VIII 44.

[183] *Fama di loro*...: Italian for "The world forgets them and their
fame." *Inferno*, III 49.

[184] *Bontà non è*...: Italian for "There is no goodness to adorn the
memory of him." *Inferno*, VIII 47.

[185] *Vedi che*...: Italian for "You can see that I am someone who
weeps." *Inferno*, VIII 36.

and blood was mixed in with the tears that streamed down the wretches' face. And there are angels here, and there are great kings there. And above all on the river Acheron, near which was the faction of the wicked, as by the dry bank of the bog, in which were those who were overcome with anger, Dante saw a boat coming down the river and through the bog, and on the boat was Charon here, Phlegyas there; and the two of them were yelling and both fell silent when they heard Virgil's voice. What was I to conclude?

XXVIII.

This, for now: that there was a kind of a helmsman of Hell like a kind of pilot of Dis, and an Ante-Inferno like an Ante-Dis, and that the souls of Ante-Inferno were similar to the souls of Ante-Dis, as Charon to Phlegyas and the Styx to the Acheron. Meanwhile, I focused my attention on the thick bunch of sinners in limbo, who say:

> *... tristi fummo*
> *Nell'aer dolce che dal sol s'allegra,*
> *Portando dentro accidioso fummo:*
>
> *Or ci attristiam nella belletta negra;*[186]

and I noted that they were in sadness similar not only to the sad souls of the indolent, but also to their companions who beat on each other, one of whom says: "I

---

[186] *Tristi fummo...*: Italian for "we were sad in the pleasant air gladdened by the sun, bearing within ourselves the slothful vapor: now we are saddened in the black sludge." *Inferno*, VII 121 ff.

am one who weeps."[187] With respect to which, I remembered that a violent person, violent against himself and his things at least, weeps when he should be
merry (*Inf.*, XI 45): which strengthened the relationship between the sinners in the fertile bog, whom I
said [were] incontinent of irascibility without injury,
and those of the seventh circle, whom I had declared
guilty of anger. But I was expecting something else:
that the people in limbo who grieved were guilty of
sloth was indubitable to me, among other reasons because *acedia* is, according to Gregory of Nyssa's definition (*S.*, 1st of the 2nd, XXX 8), "*tristia vocem amputans*,"[188] which gives an explanation not only of the
sadness of those souls that were sad already in life,
but sad also to be unable to utter their hymn with inte-
gral voice. Now, those indolent souls are certainly
similar, in their state and in their sadness, to the "*anime triste di coloro che visser senza infamia e senza
lodo.*"[189] Who, besides, were similar to the apathetic
souls, those in Purgatory: in punishment; in that they
were both incessantly running about. The apathetic
then I could consider also as the wicked or the indolent of the Ante-Inferno: whom I had seen to be similar in many ways to the incontinent of anger in the
Ante-Dis. So that I was arriving, little by little, at the
thought that the Ante-Inferno like the Ante-Dis was
populated by the apathetic. Actually, *acedia* refers to

---

[187] *Son un che piango*: *Inf*. VIII, 36.

[188] *Tristia vocem amputans*: Latin for "the sadness that cuts off the voice."

[189] *Anime triste...*: Italian for the "sad souls of those who lived without infamy and without praise." *Inferno,* III 35-36.

someone who does no good, in that acedia is defined
as "*taedium bene operandi*"[190] (*S.*, 1st of the 2nd, LXI-
II *passim*); and Virgil said of one of those soiled people, by which he meant all of them: "*Bontà non è che
sua memoria fregi.*" So, they didn't do any good [in
life]. But perhaps because the love (*Purg.*, XVII) that
attracted them to it was listless? Not exactly, but because, under the predominance of irascibility, they
loved evil. Did they do evil then? No: because then
they would have been punished among the violent.
They did neither good nor evil then, exactly like the
wicked in the Ante-Inferno, but with the difference
that these wretches were never alive, or they didn't
enjoy the freedom of will granted by God as his greatest gift, and the incontinent of anger profited by it, for
the love of evil, but did not do either good or evil
then. So that while Hell, as it is, does not receive the
former, so Dis does not want the latter. Now these
seemed to me to be for two reasons: the soul of those
conquered by anger and the souls who gurgle their
hymns; but I saw that they had something in common,
beyond being in the bog, "Tristitia";[191] which in immobile souls was signified by the very words of their
song, and in the unruly it was hinted at by offended
looks and declared with emphasis by one of them:
"*Vedi che son un che piango.*" Now, Sorrow is "in the
middle of two passions for the irascible person: given
that it follows fear; in that when the evil that one fears
occurs, sadness results; and it precedes the impulse to
anger because when someone proceeds to vengeance

---

[190] *Taedium bene operandi*: Latin for "weary to do good."

[191] *Tristitia*: Latin for "Sadness" or "Sorrow."

from a prior sadness, it involves an act of anger." (*S.* 1st of the 2nd, XXV 1). Above all I remembered: "the irate person has hope of punishing, because he desires revenge as much as possible. Whence if the status of the person who did the harm was very high, anger does not result, only sorrow" (*S.* 1st of the 2nd, XLVI 1). At this point, it seemed to me that I was looking straight at Dante and to have figured out a difference between sinners [in general] and sinners in the bog. And that was evident from the fact that the first are thick and immobile in the limbo, to show that they discount that passion of concupiscence, in other words Sorrow, the which "implies tranquility in evil" (*Summa.* 1. c.); and the second are moving and restless, to indicate that they obeyed the impulse of irascibility; but to a certain point; not having arrived at enjoying that "tranquility in a good" which is the joy of vengeance: in a good because "to cause harm is understood as a good" (*Summa.*, 1, c.). Thus did I conclude: but I still had my doubts about how they could be considered incontinent of irascibility both the immobile and the restless, seeing as the former, rather than incontinent, had to be judged deprived, as fear had gotten in the way of their acting and caused their sadness: fear which is the passion of irascibility, which is opposed to hope or desire. To that I responded that incontinence had to be interpreted as disorder or disequilibrium, and that they were thick beneath the slime and next to those who in that slime were brawling, for the same reason that in front of the incontinent of love for riches there were the prodigal, so that as either greedy or prodigal they could be content going by the same name as misers or spendthrifts, just as the tranquil and restless souls in the Styx could define themselves as unrestrained or unbalanced in the passions of irascibility. And the Poet stood above them and represented, in a very clear manner, how a man must be temperate amidst such passions. When Dante, repulsing Argenti,[192] who perhaps wanted to climb into the boat (but something else makes me doubt it, that the Dantesque episode was suggested by the Virgilian one with Palinurus: *Da dextram misero et tecum me tolle per undas*:[193] *Aen.*, VI 370 ff.) and causing Virgil to embrace him and kiss him for his disdain, declares that compassion is not always a virtue, just as anger is not always a sin; and that the impulse to become irascible is natural to man when it is according to reason (*Summa*, 2nd of the 2nd, CLVIII 2), and that there exists an appetite for laudable anger, which is called "anger through zeal, when someone desires, in accordance with reason, to exact vengeance (*vindicta*)" (ib.). And here the vengeance was, if nothing else, just, because it came from God. Now, whoever is not capable of this "anger through zeal," just as whoever is only capable of "*anger through vice*," sins, and as Dante reserves a place for great kings in that filth, per Virgil's expression, I do not know whether he meant for them to be submerged there for lack of the first, or abundance of the second.

XXIX.

[192]Repulsing Argenti: It is Dante who expresses his contempt of him, but it is Virgil who physically pushes him away from the boat. *Inferno*, VIII 31 ff.

[193]*Da dextrum misero...*: Latin for "Give a poor wretch a hand, and carry me with you over the waves."

These great kings arrested my thought. It was clear
that their castigation after death was in stark contrast
to their nobility in life, and that among the swine and
great kings Dante intended to depict the opposition
between the noblest and the vilest. And here I concluded that Dante really makes the vile the opposite
of noble, indeed he deems the vocable noble to mean
not vile almost (*Conv.*, IV 16). And he makes vile
mean the same thing as bestial (*Conv.*, III 7), saying
that he has seen "many men so vile and so low in condition that they almost appear to be beasts." Which is
even better explained by these words (*Conv.*, II 8):
"things must be denominated by the last nobility of
their form; just like man by reason, and not by the
senses, nor by anything less than what is noble: hence
when it is said: 'a man lives,' it must mean 'a man
uses his reason'; which is his special life and action
on the part of his most noble part. And yet whoever
departs from reason and uses only the sensory part, he
no longer lives as a man, but as a beast." These words
illustrate the fact that those who submit reason to lust
are, according to the Poet, like animals: lechers like
starlings and then cranes, and the two of them like
doves, in which desire precedes the will; gluttons, like
dogs; and when he says that dogs are, implicitly, like
spendthrifts whose voices sound like barking, which
is the same as saying that they didn't live like men
and consequently that they lived like animals, he declares:

> *La sconoscente vita che i fe' sozzi*
> *Ad ogni conoscenza or li fa bruni.*[194]

---

[194]*La sconoscente vita...: Italian for "The indiscriminate life that
made them filthy, makes them blind to any cognizance." Inferno,*

And on guard over the gluttonous then is the demon Cerberus, who with his three throats barks like a dog, and over the spendthrifts, Pluto, who is called a damned wolf. But the damned in the Styx are also called dogs, just as the great kings are compared to pigs: so that it can be affirmed of them as well that they did not use their reason. They were beasts then, and they will be those, even if one does not wish to say so, who were never alive, who return all the same; as Dante himself observes (*Conv.*, IV 7): "... living as a man means using one's reason. Therefore, if living is being, and in that sense departing is departing from being [i.e., from using one's reason], then departing means to be dead." Now, in precise reference to those perpetrators of vileness, the Poet says that they were never living. But if one knows that brutes are deprived of free will (*Summa*, 1st, LIX 3 *passim*) and use "only the sensorial part" (*Conv.*, VII 4) or appetite: that appetite which, according to the words of Dante "never does anything other than hunt and run away; and whenever man hunts what there is to hunt, as appropriate, and runs away from what is to be run away from, as appropriate, man is at the terminus of his perfection. Truly this appetite ought to be straddled by reason: so that like an untethered horse, if it is of a noble nature, without a good rider it does not run off on its own, and in the same way this appetite, which is called irascible and concupiscible, if it is noble, it ought to listen to reason; reason guides appetite by the reins and with the spurs; just as a good rider uses the reins when he hunts; and those reins are called

---

VII 53 ff.

temperance, which shows the limits of hunting; he uses the spurs when it runs away so as to turn it back to the place it wants to run away from; and this spurring is called fortitude, or magnanimity, or *virtu,* which shows him when to stop and when to spur (from *pungare*)." From which it follows that whoever does not use the reins of temperance when hunting, and whoever does not employ the spur of fortitude and magnanimity, is not noble, but vile, bestial, not alive. And here I noticed that not only do the concupiscible hunt and the irascible flee; but that by the one potentiality "the soul is inclined to pursue (hunt, says Dante) the things that are advantageous to it according to sense, and to run away from what is harmful"; whereas "the animal resists what denies it those advantageous things and what brings harm to it." (*Summa*, 1st, LXXXI 2). So Dante was able to find two types of vileness, with respect those who had not fled or resisted; those who were dominated by passion [which is] capable of vitiating either the concupiscible potential or the irascible potential of the soul in their attitudes of "fleeing": fleeing from sadness, first of all; from fear, second of all; given that the soul's passions are reduced to four: joy and sadness, hope and fear (*Summa*, 1st of the 2nd, XXV 4 *passim*), which Dante found expressed in the *Aeneid* (VI 733), and in his doctor, in Boethius (*Cons. Phil*. I). And I had already seen how those thick in the slime were atoning for their having been sad in life, for having been tranquil in evil, and the quarrelsome souls in the filth were punished for having been drawn to vengeance, but not having acted, out of fear. That if vengeance was just, then they were sinners for not having acted; if unjust, they were guilty for having desired it. And here, returning to the great kings, I remembered how Dante had adumbrated the office of the Prince, speaking of Henry[195] (Ep. V 3), the which, like Caesar, would have pardoned, just as Augustus castigated (*vindicabit*). Which falls under justice. Now, I concluded that what Dante desired in these great kings was precisely the sentiment of justice and what to them [was] the vilest because "not only is it vile what is not gentle, but, when descended from a good family, it is evil, even the vilest" (*Conv.*, IV 7), and for that reason they are like pigs, whose vileness being reduced precisely to their not having directed their will to being a Caesar at one time, an Augustus at another. And I was thinking that the pilot of the Styx, the Charon who journeyed to lower hell, Phlegyas, has such a ministry, because his loud voice pierced through the darkness from the pages of the *Aeneid* (VI 620): "*Discite iustitiam moniti et non temnere Divos.*"[196] So that in Dis, they are punished, those who do not acknowledge Justice, either *communiter dicta[197]* or what is called *Religio* and *Pietas;* and outside Dis, in the Styx, as beyond the Acheron, they did not use their freedom of will, those who, because of the passions of concupiscence and irascibility, did not resort to injury and did not want justice; so that on the one hand they are incontinent, like those who sub-

---

[195]Henry: Henry VII of Luxembourg (AD 1273-1313), Holy Roman Emperor (AD 1312-1313).

[196]*Discite*...: Latin for "Having been warned, learn what justice is, and do not denigrate the Gods."

[197]*Communiter dicta*: Latin for: "[justice] commonly referred to."

ordinated their reason to lust or to appetite, and on the other hand they are malicious, because they are tranquil in evil, or they were deterred from doing evil only by fear. They were, in summary, slothful in evil.

XXX.

I had seen how Dante had deemed not only as vile, but as extremely vile, the malevolent or inept kings. He says why (*Conv.*, IV 7) by the example of one person who, not having, in order to go anywhere, but to follow in the footsteps of another, "wandered and got lost among the thorns and the ruins, and went to places where he should not have." And he concludes by calling him brave, the first who found the way, and the other as not brave or vile, but rather extremely vile, who did not know how to follow the way already laid out for him. From which I deduced that, for Dante, the opposite of apathy, in addition to nobility and fortitude, was valor. But better still, I understood why the Poet indicated, among the slothful of the Ante-Inferno, "the shade of him who made through cowardice the great refusal,"[198] similar to the great kings among those in the Ante-Dis; because really and particularly apathetic is the person who, obliged to do good, refuses to exert the minimum effort; forgetting that his action is useful above all, and that his non-action is harmful to others, as Marco Lombardo demonstrates; he who loved the valor [that was] abandoned by the degenerate of the world of that period; concluding:

---

[198]The shade of him who made...: *Inferno*, III, 59-60.

*Ben puoi veder che la mala condotta
È la cagion che il mondo ha fatto reo.*[199]

And here I noticed that such demonstration is made on the terrace of anger and by an irascible, suggesting that if it is evil to go beyond anger, it is evil to remain there (and worse, from Dante's point of view). To be sure, nothing incensed the Poet more than the indolence of kings and emperors and, in general, the degeneration of men. Two passages came to mind immediately, one in Purgatory, the other in Paradise, when Dante was speaking more particularly about the kings of his time. Sordello, whose embrace had given rise to the digression in which Alberto Tedesco[200] is bitterly laid into (*Purg.*, VI 76 ff), points out, in the Vale of flowers, the Princes that sit there (*Purg.*, VII 64 ff); and his demonstration hinges on a cardinal point:

*Rade volte risurge per li rami
L'umana probitate.*[201]

In Jupiter's sphere, the luminous souls who first assumed the shape of the words, *Diligite iustitiam qui iudicatis terram*,[202] and then the head and neck of the eagle, sing in contempt of kings, the first of

---

[199]*Ben puoi veder...*: Italian for "You can perfectly well see that bad conduct is the reason for the world's offense." *Purgatory*, XVI 25 ff.

[200]Alberto Tedesco: Albert I of Habsburg (AD 1255-1308), son of Rudolf I.

[201]*Rade volte risurge...*: Italian for "Seldom does human probity rise through the branches." *Purgatory* VII 121-2.

which is Alberto, son of Rudolf who is the first king pointed out by Sordello in Purgatory. And in the passage in *Purgatory* (114 and 117) and that of *Paradise* (19, *"Che mai valor non conobbe nè volle,"*[203]) the valorous expression is read, as befitting kings. What did I conclude from these comparisons? From the fact that in Jupiter's heaven by the souls of Princes, lovers of Justice, the then-reigning Princes are condemned, I concluded that the aforesaid Princes, who did not know what valor was nor want it, were *invalorous* and caused displeasure for their lack of justice, and for this reason they were vile. But there was something else. I asked: where is the delightful Valley? and what does it signify? Meanwhile I knew what the evil streak was.[204] I read in *De Monarchia* (I 13): *notandum, quod iustitiae maxime contrariatur* cupiditas*, ut innuit Aristoteles in quinto ad Nicomachum. Remota* cupiditate *omnino nihil iustitiae restat adversum.*[205] And in the *Epistle* to Italian Princes, I read again: *nec seducat illudens* cupiditas, *more Sirennum, nescio qua dulcedine vigiliam rationis mortificans;* (*De Mon*, V 4):[206] And in the Epistle to the Florentines (5): *nec advertitis dominantem* cupidinem... *sanctissimis leg-*

---

[202]*Diligite iustitiam*...: Latin for "Love justice, you who judge on earth." *Paradise*, XVIII 91-93, from the Book of Wisdom 1:1.

[203]*Che mai valor*...: Italian for "[someone] who never knew or wanted valor." *Paradise*, XIX 126.

[204]Evil streak: the serpent. "Mala striscia," in Italian. See *Purgatory*, VIII 100.

[205]*Notandum, quod iustitiae*...: Latin for "It is to be noted that greed is most contrary to justice, as Aristotle said in the fifth book of his *Ethics.*" *De Monarchia*, I 11, Dante.

ibus, quae iustitiae naturalis imitantur imaginem, parere vetantem.[207] It was cupidity, then, and I omit much that I could add: the cupidity that is shown in malevolence (*Par.*, XV 3) and which is really our adversary, the ancient serpent that seduces. Since it is really Cupidity, which submerges mortals beneath it (*Par.*, XXVII 121), like that which makes the will iniquitous; which is the origin of all sins of injustice and which, symbolized in the Valley of the ancient serpent that bewitches and elsewhere is represented in famished beasts, in the lion that has a ravenous hunger, in the wolf, which has all the desires, that after a meal is more hungry than before, that was unleashed into the world by the invidious Enemy and for that reason is equal to the serpent. And in passing I observed that the wolf signified avarice more narrowly in *Purgatory* (XX, 10 ff); but in the *Inferno* (I 49 ff; 94 ff) it was all the more compared to avarice in the sense that Augustine gave it (*De lib. arb.*, III 17): *avaritia... non in solo argento vel in nummis at in omnibus rebus quae immoderate* cupiuntur *intelligenda est*,[208] and in the sense that Thomas gave it (2nd of the 2nd, CXVIII 2): *nomen avaritiae ampliatum est ad omnem immoderatum appetitum habendi quam-*

---

[206]*Nec seducat alludens...*: Latin for "And do not be seduced by wanton greed, which by the practices of the ineffable delights of the Sirens destroys the vigilance of reason."

[207]*Nec advertitis dominantem...*: Latin for "Nor heed dominant *greed*,... [which] prevent obedience to the most sacred laws, which are made in the image of natural justice." *Epistle* VI, 22. Dante.

[208]*Avaritia... non in solo...*: Latin for "Avarice... not only in silver or in coins, but in all things desired in excess, is what is meant."

cumque rem... quod avaritia est non solum pecuniae, sed etiam altitudinis...[209] Which leads us to Lucifer and to pride and to the origin of every sin. But the Valley, where then is it situated? Clearly it is in the Ante-Purgatory, where they linger, more or less, those who lingered unto their dying breath, those who were sinners to the last hour. And I considered, in addition to the passing of souls at death into contumacy of the Church, souls that "*movieno i piè ver noi e non pareva, sì venivan lente,*"[210] and their sudden stopping, the staying of other souls in the shadow behind the rock, "*Come l'uom per negghienze a star si pone,*"[211] and especially the attitude and expressions of Belacqua who showed himself to be more idle "*Che se pigrizia fosse sua sirocchia,*"[212] with his lazy movements and short sentences, among which these: "*Va su tu, che se' valente.*"[213] I saw moreover how, as in his crossing of the Styx, Dante tested that "anger through zeal," which in the noble or perfect man needs to exist, as he did again in the Ante-Purgatory, testing the same con-

---

[209]*Nomen avaritiae*...: Latin for "The word avarice has been expanded to include all immoderate appetite for anything whatsoever. Thus Gregory says in a certain homily that avarice is not only for money, but also for knowledge and *spirituality.*"

[210]*Movieno*...: Italian for "moved their feet in our direction, but did not appear, so slowly did they move." *Purgatory*, III 59-60.

[211]*Come l'uom*...: Italian for "like a man who stays in place on account of slothfulness." *Purgatory*, IV 105.

[212]*Che se pigrizia*...: Italian for "than if slothfulness were his sister." *Purgatory*, 4 111.

[213]*Va su tu*...: Italian for "Go up then if you are so valiant." *Purgatory*, IV 114.

cept by making Nino speak:

> ... *segnato dello stampo*
> *Nel suo aspetto di quel dritto zelo*
> *Che misuratamente in core avvampa.*[214]

Everything told me that with the necessity of staying outside the gate of Purgatory for the time that he was alive, and for thirty times the duration of their contumacy, an acedia or negligence or laziness was being punished in those souls; an acedia analogous to that which obstructed passage of the Acheron to the wretches in the Ante-Inferno, and passage of the Styx to the filthy people of the Ante-Dis. Among these apathetic or negligent or lazy or less valorous were the great kings of the Valley, notwithstanding that one of them, Sordello, says that "*D'ogni valor portò cinta la corda.*"[215] But why those Princes in the Valley? I omitted to look into it, although it appeared clear to me that this flowering valley was in relation to the muck, in which other submerged wretches had to be, or to the Jovial light where others flitted about; but I ran straightway to another passage in Dante where there was the same concept of segregation and honor, and where Dante, as if with a bound, saw noble spirits in a luminous clearing. In summary, the valley of the Ante-Purgatory led me to the noble castle in Limbo. And then I felt what seemed like a new and interrupted gust of wind from the distant land, which I wanted

---

[214]*Segnato dello stampo...*: Italian for "bearing the stamp in his face of that unwavering zeal that moderately burns in his heart." *Purgatory*, VIII 82 ff.

[215]*D'ogni valor...*: Italian for "of every merit, I wore the cord" *Purgatory*, VII 114.

to discover; and by many signs I understood that in a short while it would be in sight of the bold navigator. And the dark Minerva flashed me a smile.

XXXI.

Other spirits were in Hell whom I would have said were punished for acedia, hearing one of them say: "*Non per far, ma per non fare*"[216] (*Purg.*, VI 25). And these are in a place that is...

> ... *non tristo da martiri,*
> *Ma di tenebre solo, ove i lamenti*
> *Non suonan come guai, ma son sospiri;*[217]

hopeless sighs of desire (*Inf.*, IV 42); "*di desiderio [...] ch'eternalmente è dato lor per lutto*"[218] (*Purg.*, III 42). They later recognized the lofty sun; and for a defect (*Inf.*, IV 40), not for a mistake, they are lost, for they did not sin, although their merits were not sufficient, and among them there are besides the little innocents, honorable folk and great spirits (*Inf.*, IV 72 and 199). They are in the first circle of the abyss; before them, separated by the Acheron, above them, scarcely one step away, are only the indolent for whom free will was a useless gift. Now, I was thinking there was another place in hell where Dante

---

[216]*Non per far...*: Italian for "not for doing, but for not doing."

[217]*Non tristo di martiri...:* Italian for "not sad for martyrs, but only for tenebrae, where the laments do not sound like wails, but sighs." *Purgatory*, VII 28 ff.

[218]*Di desiderio...*: Italian for "of desire that is eternally given to them for a grief." *Purgatory* III, 41-2.

would have found the first of those to attribute intelligence to, those whom he had so desired to see: Farinata (*Inf.*, IX and X). He could tell himself that these
sinners too were in that sepulcher for no other sin
than that of not having adored or recognized the Creator and for having held that the soul dies with the
body. And then also because here they let out dolorous sighs, certainly more intense sighs than what they
let out in Limbo to stir the eternal breeze, because
that was lamentation without martyrs and here they
were true martyrs (IX 133, X 2), and wicked was the
torment and hard the moans (IX 111, 121). Nor did
the Poet neglect here, just as he had not neglected in
Limbo (IV 24), to note the darkness of the place; and
just as Cavalcante says jail is blind, Virgil says that
Limbo is sad because of the tenebrae. And from Limbo the Poets find themselves in the darkest and most
tempestuous place, just as from the cemetery of the
Epicureans they come across a crueler throng. A bad
stench is the novelty they smell first, and then perfect
obscurity and wails are what they sense. The Epicureans are within Dis, but on the terraces, just as those
who are suspended in Limbo are within Hell though
"in the first circle that surrounds the abyss." And Dis
is in the valley in a hollow of the Stygian bog, therefore almost on the same level, just as Limbo is almost
on the same level with the Acheron. And in the Stygian bog are souls scorned by Dis, just as beyond the
Acheron there are other souls disdained by Hell such
as it is: they are both slothful, even if in different
ways, the ones having been repelled by heaven, the
others by hell; and some by the hell of incontinence,
and others by that of malice. I saw these correspon-

dences and I said that there was truly a similarity between those buried in the sepulchers and those suspended in Limbo. And I noted another similarity between those on the far side of the Acheron and this
side; which consisted in this: that the suspended were
as such because they had lost their free will after the
first sin, at least according to Thomas' restriction (1st
LXXXIII 2), *non quantum ad libertatem naturalem,*
quae est a coactione, sed quantum ad libertatem,
quae est a culpa et a miseria;[219] and the wicked, who
never were alive, had become as if deprived, after
having lived like animals, which do not have free
will, unlike men or angels. So that by considering
these last two, one comes to a better understanding of
Dante's thought; given that angels from the beginning, because they were created in a state of grace,
had true merit, but some of them quickly destroyed
their prior merit (*Summa*, 1st, LXIII 5 and 6); and
"their free will being inflexible after election, even after the first instant, in which it had a natural predilec-
tion for the good, would not have posed an impediment to its beatitude, would have been confirmed in
the good." It's a matter then of a single and instanta-
neous act of free will, in which the order of angels
"broke," some choosing good, others evil. But Dante,
not following the theologians on this, adds a third
group of angels that in the act of free will did not
break rank and did not choose either good or evil; rejecting the gift of free will that God gave them. And
thus the men who, with them, are stung by big insects
and wasps. Now, nevertheless, in this defect of free

---

[219]*Non quantum ad...*: Latin for "not so much for natural freedom,
which is [a state free] from coercion, but for freedom that is [free]
from fault and misfortune."

will they are similar to those of the infernal vestibule and those of the first circle; but they are different insofar as in the first the refusal of the act of will was voluntary, and in the second, involuntary, notwithstanding that they too could be saved by believing, as others believed and were saved, in the future Christ. But in that there is a mystery which for Dante remains a mystery even in Paradise, how some were predestined and others not: what is more, we can understand how he might not judge it as totally involuntary the lack of faith in those who died before having been baptized. And thus we can understand why he puts the Limbo within Hell, which he was moreover led to do by the theologians' doctrine (*Summa suppl.*, LXIX 5). Whence the indolent and the unbaptized are similar in one way and not in another: now I asked myself in what way were they different, those of the sepulchers and those in Limbo? in that I had seen in what way they were similar. And I answered that the nonbelievers differed from the unbaptized in the same way that the unbaptized differed from those who had never been alive, in their will. The lack of faith had been totally voluntary in the ones; quasi involuntary in the others; the ones, even after Christ, did not believe; the others, although before Christianity, adored god, although not properly; and they held certain Christian beliefs, like that of the immortal soul. And the first were kings of malice given they were punished within Dis. But although the will of the heresiarchs was bad, they also, humanly speaking, focused their thoughts on doing good, and for that reason they were not placed further down, just as there was no place further up because their will was bad. In the end, I thought that only the sight of the truth makes the will free, correct, and sound (*Purg.*, XXVII 140) and that ignorance is what offends it and leads it astray; and that it can be said that all sins that originate in ignorance can be reduced to acedia (*Summa*, 1st of 2nd, LXXXIV 4). They were apathetic then, in a certain mode, both those in Limbo and those in the sepulchers. Because, as Dante expressly says (*Purg.*, XVII 130), love for the good can be lazy, as much to acquire it as to see it. Apathetic are all those in the Ante-Inferno and in the Ante-Dis, and all those in both places beyond the river and immersed in the filthy bog, apathetic with respect to the active life; those on this side of the Acheron and along the fortifications of Dis, apathetic with respect to the contemplative or intellectual life. Now, as the highest virtue of the active life and the one that completes the others is justice, which Dante calls (*Conv.*, I 12) the most proper to man and for that reason the most amiable, and declares [that] the world [is] optimally disposed (*De Monarchia.*, I 13 [sic][220]) *cum iustitia in eo potissima est*;[221] thus injustice is the worst evil. But one can omit justice and practice injustice; which especially in Princes, ministers of justice, is cowardice or crime. Now, in the filth of the Styx, as everyone is lacking in the active life, so everyone but especially the kings are punished for not having been just, which is the same as being unjust, even if they had not committed any other injustice than this, that of not having practiced justice, or that of not having been what a

---

[220]I 13: in fact, it is I 11.

[221]*Cum iustitia in*...: Latin for "when justice is strongest in it."

king should be or more generally a man acting correctly, i.e., in a just way. And here a new cause for
marvel occurred to me, not seeing all the commentators, who are in fact very few, to have accepted an
opinion by someone who exhausted his vision in the
admirable maelstrom that is the Dantesque Poem.[222]
He had correctly seen Aeneas as the Messenger of
Heaven who opened the gates of Dis with a wand,
and he had given the best and clearest reasons which I
am not going to repeat. But to me these reasons appeared indubitable, when I considered that nobody
could have been chosen by Dante to cross the Styx,
the bog of inactivity or injustice or cowardice or ignobility or disorder in irascibility; in which great kings
had been immersed; better than him who by Dante
himself is taken for a model (*Conv.*, IV 26) of the
good rider who restrains and spurs the concupiscible
and the irascible with temperance and fortitude: in the
first place, his having succeeded in leaving behind the
pleasure and delectation of Dido; in the second, his
having succeeded, alone with the Sibyl, in entering
into Hell; better than him who by Dante (*De Mon.*, II
3) is declared an example of such proper, such ances-
tral nobility, while recollecting Virgil's verses, among
which these: *Rex erat Aeneas nobis, quo* iustior *alter
Nec pietate fuit nec bello maior et armis*[223] (*Aen.*, I
544 ff.). The Messenger of Heaven was really Aeneas, and he crossed the Styx with dry-eyed laments,
as the Poets of Limbo crossed the small river like *terra firma*, so that if the canal that separates the castle

---

[222]Original foonote: Michelangelo Caetani.

[223]*Rex erat Aeneas*...: Latin for "Aeneas was our king, than whom
no one was more just in piety, nor better at war or in arms."

of wisdom from the common people is no defense against the wise, the bog of ignobility cannot retard and sink whoever is supremely noble.

XXXII.

The Poet has the sun in his eyes: he is turned toward liberty. Before him is a forest filled with odors, warmth, warbling. One week earlier he was simply looking at the sun on a hill. Now another wood is behind him. The one was a dark wood, a little less bitter than dead; the other is the divine forest, thick and alive: the one, vice and ignorance; the other, innocence and light. Dante is now in the state of soul right before sin. His reason illuminates his will, and he rides smoothly, like a free rider, his sensory appetite docile. He can in this way choose his way. But he could not on that morning that was already so far-away; because first the panther, proud with its variegated hide, then a lion *"con la test'alta e con rabbiosa fame,"*[224] and a wolf *"che di tutte brame sembiava carca nella sua magrezza,"*[225] constrained him to take another path. On this other path, Dante contemplated the effects of the three dispositions that heaven does not want: incontinence, bestiality, and malice. It appears probable to me that the three feral beasts symbolized precisely the three dispositions: the panther incontinence, the lion (Boethius writes in IV: *"Lo stemperato d'ira fremisce? animo di leone aver*

---

[224]*Con la testa*...: Italian for "with head [held] high and a ravenous hunger." *Inferno*, I 47.

[225]*Che di tutte*...: Italian for "which seemed to carry every desire in its leanness." *Inferno*, I 49-50.

si creda."[226]) bestiality or violence or anger; the wolf, which is similar to many animals and, because of Lucifer's envy, was unleashed on the world, the malice particular to man or fraud, which he had seen germinating in so many types of sin and which was the first sin of the first Angel and the first Man. The malice was double in fact, in Dante's interpretation of Aristotle: malice by force and malice with fraud: mad bestiality and malice proper so called: thus, at the foot of the hill, it came toward Dante with two faces. But it was tripartite, theologically considered; malice by force or violence or anger, malice with fraud necessarily conjoined to it, in which there is trust, or pride. And malice, thus tripartite, was symbolized perhaps on the high tower of Dis in the form of the three infernal, blood-splattered furies. Of which Alecto (*Si tibi bacchatur mens, tunc Alecto vocatur*[227] says one of the verses cited by Pietro di Dante), who weeps (scil., "*E piange là dove esser dee giocondo,*"[228] said of the violent souls or iracund with consummate injury in the *Inf.*, XI 45), it is certainly violence or anger, and Tisiphone in the middle is betrayal or pride, and Megaera fraud or envy. Now these three Furies, together with the Gorgon, turn a man to stone, like the two Feral Beasts that represent the three of them, and are both similar in "hunger," i.e., cupidity; they have

---

[226]*Lo stemperato...*: Italian for "The man given to excessive anger shudders? He thinks he has a lion's nature."

[227]*Si tibi bacchatur...*: Latin for "If your mind rages, then Alecto is summoned."

[228]*E piange là...*: Italian for "and cries there where it ought to be merry."

a consimilar effect, with the difference of the panther, which makes one turn back by its returning every now and again, but does not eliminate the hope of moving forward and overcoming the obstacle: the lion instills "fear," the wolf gives off "*tanto di gravezza con la paura che uscia di sua vista*"[229] that the Poet loses hope. And this made me believe that the two feral beasts were really equivalent to the three Furies, and that the feral beasts and the Furies symbolized what I said, and that the Gorgon amongst the Furies is "fear" amongst the feral beasts. Now then, Dante or, better yet, Man, is not free; and he turns around and goes back into the wood of ignorance and vice, of servitude that is. How distant is that other forest, the forest of freedom! distant and opposite. Reason makes itself felt in him, faintly at first, reveals itself for what it is, proposes another way to him. And Man follows it, but he has his doubts: whence Reason reveals to him that it is recommended by Faith or divine knowledge, and this was requested by Lucia, and she by Mary. Then man is satisfied. He must then visit, in order to reacquire his freedom of will, the realm of the dead. He enters into hell and in the vestibule he finds those to whom such freedom was given in vain, then into the first circle, on the other side of the Acheron, those from whom such freedom was taken away by the first sin and not restituted by the faith in Christ, come and to come. He descends to the second, the third, the fourth circle, where those in whom the will was subjected to sensory appetite are found, subjected rather to that side of themselves that is called

---

[229] *Tanto di gravezza*...: Italian for "so much concern for the fear one has on seeing it."

concupiscible: the lechers, gluttons, avaricious and prodigal. Then he finds himself on a fifth level, in a pond that grows deeper, in the middle of which is the city of Dis, the real Hell. In the ditches and in the morass around the city rumble and brawl those whose will was really turned toward evil, for excess of irascibility, but who didn't commit it, and those whose will, for lack of irascibility, didn't suppress the evil but settled into it sadly. Within the walls of Dis, they sigh heavily within their tombs, those who for malevolence rejected the faith that gives freedom. Within Dis, gradually lower, are punished those whose will turned to evil and practiced it: first those who practiced it without the aid of reason, but then with their will subjected to their appetite only; and they practiced it against their Neighbor, against themselves, against God himself and God in Nature and in Art; then those who practiced it against men with the aid of reason together with their will and appetite; finally those who practiced it, with the aforementioned aid, against God and whoever still holds God dear. Within Dis, then, there is injustice, or offense against Justice, which has two parts loftier and more sacred, Religion and Piety, as well as the injustice that offends against them, more properly called impiety and irreligion. On the perimeter of Dis, within and without, is injustice, so to speak: that is, there are those who acted properly, but who didn't acknowledge God, and those who acted poorly, but didn't acknowledge justice. Above them are those who found their good in the gratification of the senses. At the edge of hell, on either side of the Acheron, are those who acted properly but who did not acknowledge the true God, those who did not act poorly, but who do not act properly either, not having chosen between good and evil. They are all averse to God. Reason, illuminated by Philosophy, explains to man this arrangement of sins and punishments, and says then that Aristotle identified the three bad dispositions, incontinence, bestiality, malice; that incontinence is what is punished in the second, third, fourth and a part of the fifth circle, and Malice and Bestiality in the other part of the fifth, as well as in the sixth, and in the seventh, eighth and ninth circle. And continuing to linger on the wrongs contained in these rings, he declares that malice (he does not yet speak about bestiality) has injury for its end, as much to say that it is one with injustice, and this end is fulfilled either by force, whereby it is called Violence, or with fraud against someone with whom there was, or was not, a relationship of trust: a distinction made in part by Tullius. In fraud there is intelligence, which does not exist in violence, hence the latter then is called mad bestiality in Aristotelian terms. Fraud in which no trust relationship exists breaks only the chains that unite us with other humans, it offends *Humanitas*, as Tullius says; fraud in which there is a trust relationship breaks also the stricter and more sacred bonds that are maintained by *Pietas,* according to Tullius, or *Pietas* and *Religio* according to the theologians who divided the one word comprising both ideas. This is the philosophical or Aristotelian explanation. But Man has surely learnt the proper name of the special sins punished in the second, third, fourth circles, and somewhat obscurely and confusedly has felt [the need] to hint at the description of the sin punished in the fifth; with the words *carnal sinners, vice*

of lust, fault of gluttony, lack of moderation in spend-
ing, avarice, stinginess and prodigality, the souls of
those overcome with anger, the sad... bearing within
themselves a slothful vapor: sins these, with the addition of heresy, which Man had already seen when
Reason declares to him the system of punishment in
hell.

XXXIII.

And the Poet remains fixed on the sill of the fourth
ledge of Purgatory, when he asks for and obtains a
new declaration about the special Sins that are atoned
for in the ring that is before him and in the other three
that are above him. What has he seen so far? He has
seen souls completely turned to God, up on the mountain which is below the hemisphere opposite that
which arches over the earth and at the center of which
is Jerusalem. But before entering the gate to Purgatory he sees tired souls wandering slowly or sitting
down, who turned naturally to God, but tardily, for a
defect in their will. These souls are of four reasons:
the excommunicated, others who put off their penitence until the moment of death, others whose penitence was in a certain way extorted through a violent
death, others still who are kings or princes, who neglected what they were supposed to do (*Purg.* VI 92).
All are negligent, as much to say apathetic in a certain
way; and they can be reduced to two types: first, the
negligent who had, if not lost, misplaced at least, eternal love through ecclesiastical malediction, and those
who, segregated from communion with the faithful,
had been placed in the condition of the unfaithful; and

they correspond as much with those suspended in
Limbo who have lost heaven for not having faith, unless the first could turn and wanted to turn to God, but
the rest were less able and less willing to recognize
the faith, as with the heresiarchs who were able but
did not want to turn to God; and, second, the negligent who while not being in a state of infidelity, lived
averse to God and only turned to Him at the last
minute; and these correspond with the indolent of the
Ante-Inferno as well as with the other slothful of the
Styx, who lived and died averse, even though not
having caused any harm per se. Just as among them
were, like pigs in their filth, great kings, because in
them valor is the greatest duty and easier for them and
more useful for others, so among these negligent are
emperors, kings, and princes, in a pleasant Valley,
punished for some negligence which, although not
grave in itself compared to that of the other expec-
tants, is punished however with like delay, because in
their case they should have had less of it. And the
pleasant Valley corresponds however with the noble
Castle, insofar as here and there the nobles and great
spirits are segregated, whose grace, in heaven, is
gained by the honored name they have on earth (*Inf.*,
IV 76 ff). And although the correspondence does not
seem so exact, to ensure that the four kinds of indolent souls in the Ante-Inferno and Ante-Dis are recalled by the four types of negligent souls in the Ante-Purgatory, Dante's design of an external symmetry
is nevertheless seen, subdividing into four these types
that would actually be two. But he wanted the correspondence to be double: of the Ante-Purgatory with
the Ante-Inferno and Ante-Dis, as reasonably it had

to be, the Ante-Purgatory lasting for an entire life-
time, being converted only at the last moment (with
the exception perhaps of princes, whose negligence
was, on the other hand, more serious); and of the Ante-Purgatory with the Ante-Inferno and Limbo only,
in which correspondence the Valley recalls the Castle; and of the fourth ring of Purgatory with the fifth
and sixth circles of Hell. Dante climbed the three
steps, on the top step of which was the Angel, seated,
and he enters through the unbolted gate with the sev-
en *P* on his forehead,[230] where whoever has turned to
God must not look back again, and he is, from then
on only, received by him in penitence. He climbs tir-
ingly from ledge to ledge (because only when he will
have purged his guilt will his will be free and his feet
will no longer feel fatigue: *Purg.*, XII 124), and he
sees the penalty of pride paid for first, named and
qualified so many times already as the desire for excellence (XI 86); next, the sin of envy, by which one
is happier for the harm done to others than for one's
own fortune (XIII 110); by which the desires become
fixed where in company they lessen partly (XV 50);
then the fire of anger or iracundity, which by the examples of both contrary virtue and punished sin clearly fulfills a desire for vengeance. It is remarkable in
fact that the three examples of punished sin are a
impiety of a mother who kills her baby, an unsuccess-
ful vendetta of one man against another, and a suicide. No sooner has the Poet visited these three ledges
and climbed up to the fourth, then his reason makes
him want to declare that what he just saw weeping below is the tripartite love of evil; evil against one's

---

[230]P: P for *peccati*, or sins.

Neighbor; one's Neighbor, not God, not in and of Himself, because God himself cannot be hated if seen *secundum seipsum o per essentiam*[231] (*Summa*, 2nd of the 2nd, XXXIV 1), nor oneself, if the good that one wants for oneself is good, and not evil passed off as good, and if one loves oneself for what one is principally, not for what one deems oneself principally to be, *secundum naturam corporalem et sensitivam*[232] (*Summa*, 1st of the 2nd, XXIX 4). It has to do then, at this point in Purgatory, with Man, that he be what he truly has to be: *turned* to good or rather to God, who *convertit omnia ad seipsum*;[233] but only *in quantum est essendi principium, per essentiam, per seipsum*,[234] not for certain of its effects: for then Man can hate him; and hatred *est aversio quaedam*[235] (*Summa*, 2nd of the 2nd, XXXIV 1). So hatred for God and for one-self is there in the opposing barathrum, but not high up on the holy mountain. High up, the love of causing harm to one's Neighbor, taken for a good, is atoned for: the sin of errant Love. And the harm one does to one's Neighbor is loved by sinners mediately; in that immediately they love excellence, power, favor, honor and fame, vengeance or the satisfaction of their anger; but in order to reach these ends, they covet

---

[231] *Secundum seipsum*...: Latin for "actually or in essence."

[232] *Secundum naturam*...: Latin for "in one's corporeal and sensorial nature."

[233] *Convertit omnia*...: Latin for "turns all things to himself."

[234] *In quantum est*...: Latin for "insofar as He is the origin of being, in his essence, in himself."

[235] *Est aversio quaedam*: Latin for "is a kind of aversion."

their Neighbor's suppression and doing harm to him, in sum. If a man's Neighbor had actually suppressed him, and in some way harmed him, would there be sinners on the three ledges of Purgatory? Dante must not think so because then they would be perpetrators of malice, whose goal is harm, for which, having attained it either by force or by fraud, they would be *averse* from God, in Hell. And when they had not repented of it? But look: for certain sins, they would not have acted in time; for instance, if they had killed a benefactor or guest; and then, for Dante, certain sins involve a blindness and a hardening (*excaecatio et obduratio... animi humani inhaerentis malo et aversi a divino lumine*:[236] *Summa*, 1st of the 2nd, LXXIX 3), symbolized by the Gorgon who is in the three Furies' hands, which renders the repentance if not impossible, at least dilatory enough to constrain the penitents to a long stay in the Ante-Purgatory. And had they desired it only, this evil, but not committed it, did they not have for that reason the need to turn to God with repentance in order to be admitted into Purgatory? They had: otherwise, *turned* as they were toward a good, according to their thought, which not only is not a real good but an evil, according to the truth, they would have been ever *averse* from God; and they would have found themselves between those whom anger vanquished and those who were tranquil in evil. So Man, having arrived at the fourth ledge, learns that the proud, envious, and iracund of the first three rings of Purgatory, loved doing harm to their Neighbor, and he understands immediately that those of the three

---

[236]*Excaecatio et obduratio...*: Latin for "blindness and obduracy... of the human mind cleaving to evil and averse to divine light."

last circles of Hell who caused harm, not just to their Neighbor, are the iracund, envious, and proud. In Purgatory they are gradually qualified by such names, and only later left, in the ring of acedia, at the entrance, declared with a Thomistic philosophical reasoning; in Hell they are declared with an Aristotelian philosophical reasoning, before being visited, at the exit of the terrace of acedia. Therefore Man gets a sense for the definition of so-called acedia which is the sluggishness of Love in seeing or acquiring the good that is truly a good; in which definition is understood acedia in both the practical life and also the intellectual one. And he understands that this acedia is that of those *turned* to God, that what is *averse* cannot persist except in hatred, in other words in aversion, lacking in effect though, or indolent, if one wishes, of this same good. And he visits this ledge as well as the other three, in which are espied the sins of avarice and its opposite, and those of gluttony and lust, which Reason does not give a proper name to, but declares like love that is too often abandoned to a good that is not a real good, thinking almost that his disciple already knows these names there in Hell. And he reaches the living forest. From the woods to the forest: from the impediment of vice to freedom, from the tenebrae into the light.

XXXIV.

Above him is Paradise which, by merely looking into the eyes of Beatrice, in other words into Divine Knowledge, he ascends after having been immersed in the rivers Lethe and Eunoe. At first he sees the heaven of the Moon, a planet with marks on it, whose saints appear as though through transparent glass or translucid water, slightly misted over; then the heaven of Mercury, a sphere that is veiled to mortals by other rays, in which the blessed appear like fish in a tranquil and pure fishing hole. Defective had been the virtue of both the one and the other [the saints and the blessed]. The former had made holocausts of their will to God; then their will was forced. But the will, if it wishes, is not deadened, and in this then it suffered the defect of their virtue. Thus, by a mystery, also the lack of faith and because of free will in the non-believers of Limbo, it was not completely involuntary. The correspondence between these the blessed who pray and those the damned who lament is clear. The former had their will, through original sin, decided by God; the latter had united it by vow to God. The one group did not join itself to God, the other did not stop: nor by their sin: in truth, the latter are not really stuck in Hell for their punishments, nor are the former excluded from their rewards in Paradise; and nonetheless by their own fault, the ones are in the first circle of Hell, and the others are in the furthest sphere of heaven. And yet the blessed, they correspond in this way with the indolent on the other side of the Acheron: by the fact that both suppressed their will, but the ones in themselves, and the others in God. In the second realm are spirits, active albeit but because they enjoyed honor and fame. Therefore, their activity had less merit, because their desires deviated from God. In which sphere would Farinata have had his reward, he who had set his mind on doing good, if he had not denied God? In which would the quarrelsome

of the Styx, those who were not active, but were driv-
en however, although in vain, from irascibility which
has arduousness in its sights? In this: the one that corresponds with the other terrace of averse or infernal
acedia. The maculate planet and the veiled star are
like an Ante-Paradise, correspondent with the Ante-Inferno and the Ante-Dis. Does it correspond with
the Ante-Purgatory? Clearly: for in this they tarry,
those whose will was slow to turn to God and whose
desires continued to move away from true love. And
thus it can be taken for a given, that those purified of
the seven *P*, the princes in the Valley of the veiled
sphere, will shine one day, with Justinian and Romeo.
And Man rises to the heaven of Venus, where beings
filled with love are, whom the influence of that star
could have drawn into the middle of the infernal
storm or the fire of Purgatory. And in this heaven it is
remarkable how Charles Martel[237] remembers
Francesca [da Rimini], and his conversation (*"E sem
si pien d'amor che, per piecerti, non fia men dolce un
poco di quiete"*[238]) recalls the conversation of that other one (*"Di quel che udire e che parlar ti piace, noi
udiremo e parleremo a vui mentre che il vento, come
fa, si tace"*[239]), and the voice of great affection, im-
pressed, brings to mind the affectionate cry; and the
lovers' souls moving in circles, and everything else,

---

[237]Charles Martel: Charles Martel of Anjou (AD 1271-1295).

[238]*E sem si pien*...: Italian for "And it seems so full of love that, to
please you, a bit of quiet will not make it less sweet." *Paradise*,
VIII 38-9.

[239]*Di quel che udire*...: Italian for "Whatever pleases you to hear
and speak, we will listen to you and speak, while the wind
remains silent, as it does [now]." *Inferno*, V 94-96.

reproduces the rapine of the shades departed from our life by way of love.

XXXV.

The man ascends into the sphere of the Sun, where the holy doctors of the Church are, those who loved the veracious manna (*Par.*, XII 84), who grew fat on it (cf. XI 139), who were nourished on real victuals, which the human flock must nourish itself on (cf. XI 124); and who found themselves in the [sphere of the] sun because, as the greatest Minister of Nature (X 28) makes the progeny of inferior things keep coming, and without it almost every power on the earth would be dead (X 18), thus the Sun of the angels gives to the soul the only nutriment vital to it and always satisfies it (cf. X 50). How different from those scholars, nourished on light and truth, those, there below, who beneath the cursed, eternal, cold, and oppressive rain, howl like dogs! how opposite that tenebrous air to the sphere of the sun! And below him Dante hears speak of the resurrection of the flesh, as if that circle where suchlike souls hurl, who were only corporal, just flesh to fatten with food, was the right place to speak about it:

> *Ciascun ritroverà la trista tomba,*
> *Ripiglierà sua carne e sua figura,*
> *Udirà quel che in eterno rimbomba.*[240]

And here above, among the famished for spiri-

---

[240]*Ciascun ritroverà...:* Italian for "Each one shall find his sad tomb again, will take up his face and his body again, will hear what resounds throughout eternity." *Inferno*, VI 97 ff.

tual manna, among those who were in a certain way only a soul, an intellect even, to be nourished by divine knowledge, he hears speak of the same mystery (*Par.*, XIV); and as in Hell, so in Paradise, the same knot becomes untied whereby, once the flesh is revived, the blessed will have more joy, and the damned more sorrow:

> *Tutto che questa gente maledetta*
> *In vera perfezion giammai non vada,*
> *Di là, più che di qua, essere aspetta.*[241]

Thus in Hell; and in Paradise:

Come la carne gloriosa e santa
Fia rivestita, la nostra persona
Più grata fia per esser tutta quanta,[242]

with what follows and precedes. Nor perhaps is the nod to Eve without purpose:

> *... la bella guancia,*
> *Il cui palato a tutto il mondo costa;*[243]

to recall the lament that, in the circle of the greedy in Purgatory, so many prayers and tears refuses:

---

[241] *Tutto che questa*...: Italian for "although this accursed people shall never be expected, there more than here, to reach true perfection." *Inferno.* 109 ff.

[242] *Come la carne gloriosa*...: Italian for "As the flesh, glorified and sanctified, is put on again, our person shall be all the more agreeable." *Paradise*, XIV 44 ff.

[243] *La bella guancia*...: Italian for "the pretty cheek, whose fine taste and descrimination cost all the world." *Paradise*, XIII 38 ff.

Legno è più su, che fu morso da Eva,
E questa pianta si levò da esso.[244]

which shows how the idea of opposing divine knowledge to the vice of gluttony might arise; arise from
the first drama of charming paradise; given that that
tree was good to eat of and beautiful to look on and of
delightful aspect; and the Tempter had said to Eve:
"on whatever day you eat of it, your eyes will open
and you will be like Gods, knowing of both good and
evil" (Gen., III). Man climbs again, and finds himself
in the heaven of Mars, where warriors of the Faith rejoice, those generous with their blood: where, no
sooner than arrived, he makes a holocaust to God, or
rather a sacrifice of his complete self. The lights sing a
holy melody: Rise and conquer. The Poet exclaims:

Ben è che senza termine si doglia
Chi, per amor di cosa che non duri
Eternalmente, quell'amor si spoglia![245]

Of course, he recalls that expiatory soul
which, contrite, says:

Vidi che lì non si quetava il core;[246]

-----

[244]*Legno è più...*: Italian for "The tree whose fruit was bitten by
Eve is higher up, and this lament originates from there." *Purg.*,
XXIV 116 ff.

[245]*Ben è che...:* Italian for "It is fine that he, who for the love of
something that does not last forever, should endlessly lament a
love that he is deprived of." *Paradise*, XV 10 ff.

[246]*Vidi che lì...:* Italian for "I saw that the heart does not grow quiet
there." *Purgatory*, XIX 109.

that soul that lies supine and extended on the ground with the others, who were avaricious, clinging to the pavement, so that their eyes are not turned upward, fixed as it were on earthly things, on things that do not last. And they are immobile and bound, those souls, just as those of Paradise are extremely mobile because of the depicted cross, the sign of the supreme sacrifice:

> *Di corno in corno e tra la cima e il basso*
> *... scintillando forte*
> *Nel congiungersi insieme e nel trapasso.*[247]

Nor are the words of Cacciaguida vain, either when he describes the quiet life of Florence within the ancient circle, without luxury, without immoderate expense, or when he speaks of Can della Scala who, depicted being born on the strong star of Mars, will show the first signs of such influence in not caring for money and will make such magnificence to conquer the silent envy of enemies. And Man is in Jupiter now, on the sphere of justice, in the heaven of just kings; who recall the great kings that have to be dipped in the filth of the Styx and in this way they remember them by their words. They glitter up there in the eye of the Eagle, two spirits, Trajan and Ripheus, who were Christians in the guise of Gentiles, and their presence is a reproof to those Christians who by not being just or by not having faith rendered the sacrifice of the Cross useless in itself. And this is like a middle paradise, assigned to virtue, of the spheres of

---

[247]*Di corno in corno...:* Italian for "From end to end and from top to bottom the lights moved, scintillating strongly as they came together and passed each other." *Paradise*, XIV 109 ff.

Venus, Sun, Mars, and Jupiter, which the soul is to employ the noblest parts of, suffers "*mistura alcuna*" of desire, which no longer has a place in the full use of beatitude, which is speculation (cf. *Conv.*, IV 22). It would seem then to cease at this point, the correspondence of rewarded virtues with punished or purged vices, and in the heaven of justice to be the antithesis of all the sins of injustice; and thus it ceases and thus it exists. Indeed, formally, the correspondence continues. In opposition to the little circle and to the ledge of violence and ire, and of course the heaven of Saturn; of Saturn, the mythical king of peace; splendor,

> *Che sotto il petto del Leone ardente*
> *Raggia mo misto giù del suo valore,*[248]

which is perhaps intended to signify that the influence of the fire of anger can descend from this planet, according to its conjunction. In any case, Saturn is the star of rustics and pacific men, not that of contemplatives. And the antithesis of Malebolge and the ledge of envy seems to be the realm of Gemini, wherein Dante recognizes his genius, Dante who, even in Purgatory (XIII 133), professes to have little offended God by envy. Turning away from that sphere of the fixed stars with its eternal Twins, Dante lowers his eyes and sees

> *L'aiuola che ci fa tanto feroci,*[249]

---

[248]*Che sotto il petto*...: Italian for "which under the Lion's burning breast shines light below, now mixed with its valor." *Paradise,* XXI 14 ff.

and on the ledge of envy I heard it said to Virgil:

> *Chiamavi il cielo e intorno vi si gira,*
> *Mostrandovi le sue bellezze eterne,*
> *E l'occhio vostro pure a terra mira.*[250]

And at the center of the cavity is situated the Prime Mover, from which the movement begins that quiets it. And there Beatrice utters the anathema against cupidity which is the cause of corruption of the human will, so that Faith and Innocence are no longer to be found except in little children in whom desire does not yet wage war against reason and will; and the same person, reasoning about the creation of angels and of the universe, declares:

> *Principio del cader fu il maledetto*
> *Superbir di colui, che tu vedesti*
> *Da tutti I pesi del mondo costretto.*[251]

In the end there is the Empyrean and in the Empyrean there is the one and trinitarian God: to contemplate whom it is necessary to have dissolved all clouds of mortality and for this it is necessary to turn to Mary

---

[249]*L'aiuola che...*: Italian for "the plot of earth that makes us so fierce." *Paradise*, XXII 151.

[250]*Chiamavi il cielo...*: Italian for "Heaven calls you and circles round you, showing you its eternal beauties, and yet your eyes only see the earth." *Purgatory*, XIV 148 ff.

[251]*Principio del cader...*: Italian for "The cause of the fall was the accursed pride of him whom you saw constrained by all the weight of the world." *Paradise*, XXIX 55 ff.

Umile ed alta più che creatura.[252]

Dante's design, – I have already glimpsed it.
The contours of his vision were clear to me.

XXXVI.

Of Dante's Poem then, I can now say that I know a
part of it that was little or poorly known: the moral
construction. The subject of which is Man, who is exposed to reward or punishment according to the good
or evil that he merits. But he cannot merit good or
evil if whoever liberates does not have the will; so
that the Poem can be called the drama of the human
will and divine justice. The latter is impenetrable
(*Par.*, XIX), the former free (*Par.*, V 19 *passim*), always and in every way. Nor do celestial influences
have so much power to annul or diminish the freedom
of the one nor consequently the reason for the other:
the mind is subject only to God and in that the will
gains its light; all the more so as the direction or
guide of the two Suns was allotted by God to men on
earth, in order to show the two ways, of the world and
of God (*Purg.*, XVI). God made man free, just as he
had made the Angel before him free. The Angels
were made together with the world, and once created
they made a choice between good and evil, and to
good and evil, once chosen, they adhered then with
full and firm will (*Par.*, XXIX). Among them some
did not choose between good and evil and did not
profit by the greatest gift that God could make, and

---

[252]*Umile ed alta...:* Italian for "humbler and greater than any
creature." *Paradise*, XXXIII 2.

"non furon ribelli nè fur fedeli a Dio, ma per sè foro."[253] The faithful Angels immediately began their art of rallying round their Creator, and the disloyal and the neutral angels, in the very attempt to rise above God, were cast down. At the very moment that the heavens began to tremble, the barathrum of Hell opened up to receive Lucifer and his companions, and the mountain of Purgatory rose (*Inf.*, XXXIV 121 ff). Man was made free and placed on the top of this mountain, in an earthly paradise. Now, he also, a small time after his creation, after seven hours, was able to make a choice, and, seduced by the evil Angel, he chose evil (*Par.*, XXVI 139). In this way, man learnt about death, and in the very act of raising himself above God he was cast down, and he populated the Earth when alive and Hell when dead. Without inhabitants' voices, in the austral hemisphere, the mountain rose high up out of the waters, on the summit of which the forest of life and innocence grew verdant. Man's will was no longer free; but it was also not, like that of the king of Angels, firmly set on evil: in that God wanted to redeem Man, incarnating himself and shedding his blood for him, and whoever already had faith in this mysterious promise expected, in Hell naturally but also in a secret place, in the first circle of it, that it should be fulfilled and that he should rejoin God. And the promise was fulfilled, and on an opposite mountain, acrosss from the deserted mountain, dangled from a tree the Man-God; and the doors of Hell were staved in, and the spheres of Heaven were populated. Since then, human will,

---

[253]*Non furon ribelli...*: Italian for "They were not rebellious, nor faithful, but stood apart." *Inferno*, III 38-39.

which even from the beginning had not been completely decided by God because it could turn around
on its own with faith in the coming Christ, turned, after baptism, and with faith in the come Christ, completely free; and everyone could merit both good or
evil. And Hell continued to receive as many as turned
their back on God, and Heaven as many as turned
their face to God; and the mountain of Purgatory saw
climbing up its terraces as many as had converted to
God after having been turned, either to evil, or to
good which is not truly good. Now, Dante wanted to
describe this triple realm of the dead. Philosophy and
Theology spoke to him about it. He wanted to show
that they were not in contradiction, provided that the
second moved the first, and that it corrected it. The
Poet, from one after the other, from this one now and
from that one later, knew that the heavens were nine
in number, with the Empyrean being the tenth, which
is pure light; that the evil that Man can do is reduced
to the seven capital sins; three of which are dispositions that heaven does not want. He thought that the
three Aristotelian dispositions had to comprise the
seven Gregorian sins. He pointed out the realms
where the seven sins were punished with eternal or
temporal torture in such a way that they corresponded
with each other through and through and that they
corresponded with the nine spheres of Heaven
through and through.

XXXVII.

Dante then thought:

The three dispositions shown by Philosophy

are incontinence, bestiality, and malice. Incontinence is to subject the reason to appetite. Appetite (or desire) has two parts: concupiscence and irascibility. There is, then, the incontinence of concupiscence and of irascibility. Not to rein in concupiscence is the aforementioned sin of lust and gluttony; and, by many if not by everyone, of avarice. But incontinence of irascibility, what is that? Anger, say the Theologians (*Summa*, 2nd of the 2nd, LXXIII 2), belongs with those sins that aim at causing harm to one's neighbor; therefore it is the sin of malice. Indeed, malice is to do harm, that is, to sin against justice; and harm, as one reads in Tullius, can be done in two ways: by force or with fraud. Anger therefore will be harm done by force. But opposed to justice, one also reads (cf. *Moralium dogma* in Sundby, *Brunetto Latini*, pp. 401 and 426), is *Truculentia* which is divided into *Vis* and *Fraus*, similar to *Negligentia*, and *Negligentia* means *non propulsare iniuriam*.[254] To which of the seven sins is this *negligentia* more similar than to acedia? In fact, acedia is *Tristitia quaedam*;[255] and, as the Doctor says (1st of the 2nd, XLVI 1), when the person who received the injury was very important, not *Ira* but *Tristitia* follows. Now, these sad, these negligent, these apathetic people would be perhaps incontinent of irascibility? Just the opposite: because irascibility is given to us in order to overcome and conquer what might bring harm to ourselves; and people like them, not only do they not have it in excess, are incontinent of it in other words, but have little or none. But, to

---

[254]*Non propulsare iniuriam*: Latin for "not to repel harm."

[255]*Tristitia quaedam*: Latin for "a kind of sadness."

step back for a moment, if the avaricious are rightly
considered incontinent in their love for riches, conceived of as a physical good, can the prodigal be
called incontinent by the same logic? It does not seem
so: and yet the prodigal have to be punished in Hell
and in Purgatory in the same place as the avaricious.
Now, with the sad whom I mentioned, which sinners
should be treated in the same way as the prodigal with
the avaricious? Clearly, the incontinent of irascibility,
or rather those who did not know how to rein in that
part of their sensory appetite; and just as ill spenders,
avaricious and prodigal both, are considered incontinent, so too the inordinate in irascibility, those who
had too much as well as those who had too little,
should be considered incontinent. But they are sad,
the negligent and slothful are: by what right can they
too be called apathetic? By this: they did not cause
harm, because if they had they would be guilty of
malice. They were not malicious then. Were they
good? No; because they were incontinent. Therefore,
they were neither good nor bad, just like the apathetic; for that reason, acedia is *taedium operandi*.[256] But
if they had really done neither good nor evil, completely in vain would have been for them the divine
gift of freedom, and they would have been similar to
the Angels who were neither rebellious nor loyal.
And the world has a great number of suchlike, whom
one could say were not alive. Now, it cannot be said
that the former offend justice, while it can be said that
the latter who are incontinent of irascibility do, because they did not do harm, but they wished to; or,
closing themselves up in indolent Sadness, they did

---

[256] *Taedium operandi*: Latin for "weariness of acting."

not reject harm. There is therefore the acedia of someone who does not choose between good and evil, and
the acedia of someone who chooses either good or
evil, but does not do it for cowardice or for the weariness of acting. But is acedia merely the weariness of
acting? No, in that beyond what may be defined as a
love slow to follow the highest Good, there is another
which can be called a love slow to see it: that to
which all ignorance is reduced. Apathetic then are
those who did not recognize or failed to recognize
God: Virgil, for example, and Farinata. To the same
degree? No: because, although the ignorance of either
an ancient great spirit, or a small innocent child that
died before baptism, is not completely voluntary (as
God alone knows); malicious, in addition to voluntary, is the ignorance of ancient and recent Epicureans, who make the soul of the body dead. Malicious-
but given that malice has harm as its end, malicious to
one's Neighbor? Now, did they inflict harm, did they
do evil to their Neighbor, these Epicureans? If they
had done harm or evil, they would not be slothful or
voluntary ignorants only, but having truly afflicted
another person by their work, they would have to be
called something else: disseminators of scandal and
schism, for example. Thus, those who not only loved
riches excessively, but who, for gold or silver, adul-
terated the things of God, they are not merely incontinent, nor can they simply be called greedy, but given
that they did evil to their Neighbor, kicking down the
good and lifting up the depraved, they ought to be included among those who use malice, and, in fact,
malice with fraud. And so too with the lustful who rejected the generation of children, and the avaricious

who refuted working the earth, they are not simple lechers and greedy people. But what are they?

XXXVIII.

And Dante said:

The subject of the Poem is not this or that man, but Man. Let us read the first stories of Man, which are in Genesis. In what way did he sin, damning all his people with him? He sinned for pride, like the wicked Angel. Why? Because he wanted to impose himself on God, transgressing his precept, which was the only precept and which contained the only sign of the subjection of Man to God. As soon as the sin was committed, he fell, forever, like the Angel; because that lifting up of himself was a lowering of himself, and pride drags down, just as humility lifts up, not only according to Saint Augustine but also Saint Gregory (*Mor.*, XVI 35, XVII 37, XXXIV 16). Now, this pride which is expressed in the desire to rise above God and which is followed immediately by a fall, – does it also occur in Adam's sons? When Adam's sons commit one of those sins by which they refuse to recognize every law and consequently every superiority of God, leaving nothing intact of divine rule, those are certainly the sins of pride, and it is reasonable to believe that they are punished immediately. And whoever violates the simplest precept and recuses himself from doing the least of what God asks of men, does he not disregard God and annul all his rule? And the simplest precepts are the first three in the Decalogue, to which must be added, according to theologians, the fourth. In these is the least that God

asks of men; and whoever recuses himself from following it is guilty of pride. But the precepts of the
Decalogue are all commandments of justice, with the
first three belonging to that part of justice which is
called religion, and the fourth to that other which is
called piety; all, however, belonging to justice;
whence whoever violates them acts against justice,
commits injury in other words. Now, injury is the
goal of malice; so that one could say that pride is the
sin of malice. But malice afflicts others either by
force or with fraud: with which of the two does this
sin of malice that is called pride afflict others? Fraud
is man's particular evil, because it is accomplished
with the intellect, and the intellect does not belong to
animals but to man. Now, the intellect certainly entered into the sin committed by Lucifer, that by
Adam, and that by the Giants, all proud beings. And
besides the intellect, what else played a part? The will
turned to evil and sensory appetite, even though in
Lucifer sensory appetite was *metaphorice* only. It is
possible then that pride is malice by fraud, given that
in pride there is intellect, and fraud cannot exist without intellect. But is that really true? Because to violate
the first four commandments is to break the special
bond that unites us to God and to whoever continues
to take after God, given that violation is always fraud,
because from benefit derives trust, the abuse of which
by committing harm is the equivalent of using fraud.
In fact, because a greater trust is generated the stricter
the bond is, the fraud will be more serious yet. Therefore pride is malice with fraud, and with a more serious fraud than other merely fraudulent malice. What
is this other fraudulent malice that is less serious than

what can be called *betrayal* in the act by Judas, who
with a kiss betrayed (*tradidit*: cf. the Gospels) the
God-Man to the Jews? What is it? Let us turn to Genesis. The proud, and therefore *envious*, devil was the
depraved counsellor of Man. His envy was made
manifest in that depraved counsel. He mutated into a
serpent, used mellifluous words, seduced, lied, deceived, separated man from God. It is also the invidiousness of Adam's offspring that performs such operations; anyone then who harms his neighbor, other
men; because envy is among equals. And then the
theologians posit a great similarity between pride and
envy, saying that from the evil done to others, which
both pride and envy lead to, they hope the proud man
might earn excellence or pre-eminence, and the envious man might stop fearing to lose the good that he
possesses. Now, also, malice with more serious fraud
is similar to that with less serious fraud, as pride is to
envy; and they differ in this that the first malice abus-
es a special trust, which derives from a special bond,
while the second must overcome the other rather languid one, which cannot even be called trust, which
derives from the broader and looser bond that binds
men to men. Whence it can be affirmed that as the
malicious with special fraud are sadder sinners, the
others must be more cunning deceivers; and that
while the first can initially appear more violent than
fraudulent, like the rebellious Angel and the proud
Giants, the second always appear in the vile shape of
the serpent that cautiously slithers. And even envy,
which fears, differs in that from pride which hopes.
Envy is therefore the malice that harms its Neighbor
while pride is the malice that injures God and which

is more similar to God; and the first offends humanity, the second piety, as Tullius says, or rather religion and piety, as the theologians specify. And with fraud they are both, and for this reason with the intellect, and they have to be signified with the symbols of three bodies and three heads: Geyron and Lucifer. But the intellect is missing in another malice that injures others, both Neighbor and God, by force. Given that the intellect is missing, malice by force or violence can be called mad; it can also be called bestiality, because there is no principal element that distinguishes man from beasts; there is of course the will, but it is subject to appetite and therefore it is almost as if it does not exist, as in beasts; and because such sin consists in appetite alone and the will subject to it, it will have the symbol of two natures, one bestial, the other human: Minotaur, Centaurs, Harpies. Now, such sin is called anger by the theologians, which is a fleeting madness, in which the intellect barely enters in order to shed a light on a wrong and an enemy, and then immediately the light goes out, leaving the vengeance to be accomplished in the dark. This blind cupidity also presses against us; to kill our life, when it is anger itself, in other words when it is malice; as if to offend our flesh with its teeth, when it is acedia turned to evil, in other words when it is incontinence of irascibility; against us as well as against one's Neighbor and against God. As pointed out by an author who is highly recommended to be consulted in such speculations (*Hugh of Saint Victor: Alleg. in Matthew*, *2:16*) saying: *Superbia... aufert homini Deum, Invidia aufert ei Proximum, Ira aufert ei seip-*

sum.[257] Mad anger, without intellect, operates differently from envy or pride: against its Neighbor, injuring him with ruthless and unjust vengeance; against God, cursing him and disrespecting him, but only with feeling or rather under the domination of irascibility. For this reason the irascible toward God are not those who abuse by a benefit of theirs, like the proud do, but those who rebel against a condemnation that they hold to be unjust or a benefit that they take as maleficent. And thus does the aforementioned author mean (*Hugh of Saint Victor, l.c.*) : *Superbia... dicit, Deum non bonum esse, Invidia et Ira dicunt non benefecisse: illa, quia alii bonum contulit, ista, quia sibi malum intulit.*[258] Therefore with the blasphemers who deny God in an impiety of grief are united those who refuse to procreate and to work, rejecting the two sweet commandments that, given by God in his goodness to the first Man before his sin, sounded lugubrious after the first sin, like a condemnation pronounced by him in his justice, and honestly an injury that those sinners wanted to avenge themselves of. And on this topic there is still the necessity to read the holy book, Genesis. In as much as that book accords with the *Physics* of Aristotle, just as *Ethics* corresponded, almost exactly, to the theological books treating of the division of sins. Since malice is made up of the three spiritual sins, given that anger is more

---

[257] *Superbia... aufert homini Deum...*: Latin for "Pride separates God from men, Envy separates one's Neighbor from him, Anger separates him from himself."

[258] *Superbia... dicit, Deum...*: Latin for "Pride... says, God is not good, Envy and Anger say He has not benefited them: the former because he brought good to others, the latter because he brought evil upon himself."

properly what Aristotle (incorrectly interpreted) calls
bestiality; and the symbols of this trigeminal malice,
which Tullius' *De Officiis* contains the idea of, are the
Furies who have with them the Gorgon which blinds
men and turns them to stone; and incontinence is
made up of the three carnal sins. What remains is the
sin in the middle, acedia, which partakes of both action and contemplation, and depends on either the
lack of will or a will turned to evil. The first is, in
both its active and contemplative natures, scorned by
God's mercy and justice; the second is punished by
God's justice because it is contrary to justice. Now
this second acedia, through its active nature, is incontinence of irascibility, and through its contemplative
nature it is malice. The apathetic for lack of will, voluntary or involuntary, are not included in the three
dispositions, for honestly they must not be included in
Hell. These three dispositions are symbolized by the
three Feral beasts: the panther, incontinence; the lion,
bestiality; the wolf, fraudulent malice. And like bestiality and fraudulent malice they have two things in
common, including cupidity, which ruins mortals,
taken in that broader sense of the term in which theologians use it (*Summa*, 1st of the 2nd, LXXXIV 1
passim); cupidity which is the origin either of excellence or of other temporal goods or vengeance; and
the blindness or hardening symbolized by the Gorgon,
which are the effect, insofar as the punishment follows immediately after the crime for the most serious
of these sins; thus the lion and the wolf are both
ravenously famished and fear is felt on the mere sight
of them, but the wolf in particular makes one lose
hope.

XXXIX.

And Dante pointed out:

Nine are the heavens of paradise plus the empyrean: nine are the rings of Hell, plus the terrestrial superficies together with the untamed wood. Because the sins are seven, one of them, acedia, should be punished in three rings according to its different types. There is a fourth type, that of the wretched who were never alive on Earth, where they came in vain, and they remain in the vestibule; they remain there to run and run, perpetually, in punishment for their indolence. So on each bank of the Acheron, although not exactly at the same level, there are two types of souls apathetic for lack of will, whose mercy and justice it either absolutely contemns or cannot accept the one and must not punish the other. In the same way, within and without Dis, which is the hell of malice, there are two other kinds of apathetic souls corresponding to the first two, malefactors in action and malefactors in contemplation; different from the first two inasmuch as here the will is not lacking but was turned to evil and offended justice, without doing harm however. So the apathetic around Dis correspond to those around the Acheron, nor perhaps for any other reason than for this correspondence, the indolent run outside hell, and the unbelievers and the baptized sigh within hell; nor perhaps for any other reason did the angels, neither rebellious nor faithful, fall from heaven. Below the two pairs of apathetic souls are the sinners of incontinence, in the three rings of upper hell; in lower hell, also in three rings, those of malice (whose bes-

tiality is the first kind). The Styx resembles the
Acheron; Phlegyas, Charon; the filthy who never
leave the bog, the indolent who never cross the river:
the latter not worthy to cross it, the former not worthy
to exit it, because the ones did not commit any good
or evil and the others naturally adhere to evil, but did-
n't do any, or rather they acknowledged what is good,
but didn't act on it. Similar to the noble Castle where
great Spirits sadly sigh, the city of Dis, along whose
terraces heavily sigh even men who put their minds to
doing good, men like Farinata and Frederick II, for
the most part worthy of the admiration and respect of
many. The two types of acedia included in the ternary
of incontinence and that of malice belong, the first, to
the incontinence of those who either did not moderate
or did not have irascibility, and the second to the malice of those who maliciously disregarded God. Of the
first group there is no good to tell, and of the second
nothing evil. And Paradise with its nine spheres recalls Hell with its nine rings; the blessed, in the heav-
en of the Moon and that of Mercury, recall the indolent for lack of will and those that had a will turned to
evil; those filled with love in the heaven of Venus recall the lechers of the second ring, and Charles Martel
recalls Francesca; the famished for true manna who
rejoice in the sphere of the sun recall the gluttonous
beaten by the rain in the tenebrous air of the third
ring, and in that heaven as in this ring the resurrection
of the flesh is spoken of; God's combatants in the
heaven of Mars bring to mind those of the fourth ring,
who lost God for the love of something that does not
last, and who praise, in contrast to the prodigal and
the greedy, parsimony and liberality; and the heaven

of justice makes one think of the bog and of the city of injustice, and the just kings recall the great kings who feared to practice justice and let themselves be contemned; and mild Saturn is placed opposite the circle of violent souls, and from the Twins the gaze falls to the plot of earth dominated by envy; and in the Crystalline Sky malediction rings out to cupidity which is the root of all sin and to pride which was the origin of the fall of the Angel and of Man's damnation. Purgatory reproduces, as a mountain can reproduce an abyss, Hell. It should have seven terraces for the seven sins in the same order as Hell, but the fourth of the one matches the fifth and sixth of the other, including acedia like indolent love, in order to see and to follow the Good. In this correspondence the fifth and sixth ring of Hell are almost on the same level and one and the same. After the souls turned to God make their way up through the terraces of Purgatory, their aversion is canceled with their sins, and thus they might purify the one conversion to a commutable good in the place destined for it. Given the partitions in Purgatory have to be nine as well, an Ante-Purgatory is added to the seven terraces for those averse from God if only a short while before death, for those blinded temporarily (*Summa*, 1st of the 2nd, LXXIX 4); and these are of two types, those who are excommunicated, and those who are not; indeed, because the types of acedia in hell are remembered to be four, the second type of them is reduced by a third; and because the noble Castle of great Spirits is recollected by analogy and by contrast, the slime of the great kings is, in that Ante-Purgatory, the pleasant Valley where princes sleep in the open air, those who were perhaps not equal to their great office, but who were nonetheless remembered, or better, even though negligent of their eternal salvation, they left behind an honorable name for themselves; and the Ante-Purgatory corresponded also with the Ante-Paradise, and Manfred reminds one of Piccarda and the princes in the Valley of the active Spirits of Mercury. And Cato, presiding over the Ante-Purgatory, showed what the four human virtues, in his necessary infirmity of will, through the freedom of that same will, could do to a pagan illuminated by the sun: reject life. Whereas a believer, moving from the untamed wood of servitude, preserving his will from evil dispositions that heaven does not want, and purifying himself of the love of evil, of the indolent love of the good, of the excessive love of the good that is not good, can climb gradually up the mountain and arrive at the divine forest, and have a free, perfectly sane will; and then ascend to the Empyrean. Wood, forest, Empyrean: complements of the nine in the three Cantos of the *Divine Comedy*.

Epilogue

One aspect then of the dark Minerva has been illuminated. The light that shines on it is certain to expose
what still remains in the shadows and half shadows of
the Poem. And it is permissible from now on to hope
that after having resolved a principal and essential
part of Dante's thought, the ethical construction of the
very great, indeed divine, expression of his thought,
just how vast and profound Dante's thought is will be
revealed to us. We can meanwhile with the aforesaid
determination circumscribe, and therefore judge, and
know, the entirety of his studies and his sources. And
this knowledge will be such a step forward that very
little space will remain between us and the goal.

Appendices

Clarifications and Additions

I.
Heaven's Messenger

No declaration of controversial passages in the *Divine Comedy* is happier than that by Michelangiolo Caetani, Duke di Sermoneta, who says that Aeneas is the messenger of heaven who opens the doors of Dis Pater. He demonstrates (*Tre chiose di Michelangelo Caetani, duca di Sermoneta, nella Divina Commedia, by D.A.*, third edition, Rome, Salviucci, 1881) first that the messenger cannot be an angel because an angel of Paradise cannot descend into hell; because the first angel described by Dante in *Purgatory* shows himself to be quite different, and must be received with other signs of respect. And the first angel ever seen by Dante on his journey is revealed by the following words spoken in *Purgatory*: *Omai vedrai di sì fatti ufiziali.*[259] Nor to an angel, who *sdegna gli argomenti umani,*[260] does the wand belong; nor the comparison to impetuous wind and to the grass snake; nor the waving of his left hand; nor his speaking to the demons of fate or Cerberus; nor his departure like a man under pressure by other concerns. Excluded then that the messenger be Mercury or the Redeemer (ab-

---

[259]*Omai vedrai*...: Italian for "From now on you will see what the officials [of heaven] look like." *Purgatory,* II 30.

[260]*Sdegna gli argomenti*...: Italian for "scorns human arguments." *Purgatory,* II 31.

surd opinions in themselves), he figures out who he can be. Already in the first colloquy, Virgil tells Dante that he was the singer of that righteous son of Anchise, and Dante responds to Virgil remembering even Aeneas who went alive into the underworld, and concludes with these words: *I am not Aeneas, I am not Paul.* Then, in front of the gates of Dis, Virgil says that Such a one had been offered to him, who certainly could not have been from anywhere but Limbo, the place of his residence, that it could be none other that Aeneas who had several times already descended through *umbram perque domos Ditis*,[261] having in hand the *venerabile donum fatalis Virgae*.[262] That confirms what Virgil says: that *from there* to the first gate of Hell was such a figure that descended the slope. "The question, that Dante made to Virgil: Whether any one of them from the first circle of Limbo ever descended into that infernal depth, was in response to the words by Virgil, which he had said to him: Such a one having been offered to him for the opening of Dis; none other could this be than some one of his consorts in Limbo, who was related to that opening and to Virgil: and this must be Aeneas without a doubt."

The doctrine hidden under the cover of strange verses is "that Aeneas must serve as the providential instrument of the opening of Dis... in order to signify all the events that prepared for the true open-

---

[261] *Umbram perque*...: Latin for "among the shadows and houses of Dis."

[262] *Venerabile donum*...: Latin for "the venerable gift of the fated wand."

ing made by Him who lifted the great prey up out of the upper circle of Dis." And that is confirmed by passages in the *Convito* and *De Monarchia*. To the objection that Dante didn't recognize Aeneas, when he showed up to open the gates of Dis, while he had already seen him among the great spirits, the Duke responds by pointing out, quite reasonably, the smoke-filled obscurity of the place; but he would have done better, it seems to me, if he had denied what Dante said, when he said that he didn't recognize him, and said instead what was contained in the verse

ben m'accorsi ch'egli era del ciel messo,[263]

which is perhaps more to the point: I saw in that the proof that Aeneas was really the messenger of providence; whereby it occurred to me that such an unknown person was a celestial agent. And his turning to his Master, to the singer of the *Aeneid*, indicates precisely his sudden desire to reconfirm with him something said by him:

... E quei fe' segno
ch'io stessi cheto ed incinassi ad esso;[264]

in that Dante wanted to speak and says: *Ora vedo...*[265]

Now, with this rectification and with every reserve with respect to the symbolic signification of the

---

[263]*Ben m'accorsi...*: Italian for "I realized that he was heaven's messenger." *Inferno*, IX 85.

[264]*Ed quei fe' segno...*: Italian for "and he made a sign that I should be quiet and bow to him." *Inferno*, IX 86-7.

[265]*Ora vedo...*: Italian for "Now I see..."

episode, I ask how ever did so evident a demonstration not pass into the Dantesque lore and into common commentary. To this I add what Virgil says:

> ...*già di qua da lei discende l'erta,*
> *passando per li cherchi senza scorta,*
>
> *tal che per lui ne fia la porta aperta;*[266]

who then adds:

> *... Tal ne s'offerse!*
> *Oh! quanto tarda a me ch'altri qui giunga!*[267]

and Dante expresses his doubt, asking whether anyone can descend from Limbo. The commentators understand here that Dante doubts not that an auxiliary was coming from Limbo, but that Virgil should be allowed to pass into Dis. The truth is that Virgil shows that he interprets Dante's doubtful question in this way,

> *Ben so il cammin: però ti fa securo.*[268]

But before anything else, let us interpret correctly Virgil's interrupted speech:

---

[266]*Già di qua...*: Italian for "and already now from there it descends the slope, passing through the circles without escort, such a one as will clear the way for us." *Inferno*, VIII 128-30.

[267]*Tal ne s'offerse...*: Italian for "Such a one has offered his help. Oh, how long he makes me wait!"

[268]*Ben so il cammin...*: Italian for "I know the way, so rest assured." *Inferno*, IX 30.

Pure a noi converrà vincer la punga,
cominciò ei, se non... tal ne s'offerse!
oh! quanto tarda a me ch'altri qui giunga!²⁶⁹

He says this after having listened attentively because, in the snow, he could not see very far. Now, the sense of his words appears to me to be this: "We need to fight and win this *on our own* (v., for example, *Inf.*, XXV 39: *Ed intendemmo pure ad essi poi²⁷⁰*), unless... he is coming as promised; and he is not such a one as to fail to arrive. But how long he takes!" Dante was frightened by this talk, because

... traeva la parola tronca
forse a peggior sentenza ch'ei non tenne;²⁷¹

that is, he understood that the conditional *unless...* expressed an actual negation, and was not reassured

con l'altro che poi venne,²⁷²

or rather with *Tal ne s'offerse.* Therefore, Dante's question is natural, wondering whether anyone *from the first circle* could descend

---

²⁶⁹*Pure a noi...*: Italian for "We have to win this fight," he began, "if not... Such a one has offered his help. Oh, how long he makes me wait!" *Inferno*, IX 7-9.

²⁷⁰*Ed intendemmo...*: Italian for "and we listened only to them then."

²⁷¹*Traeva la parola tronca...*: Italian for "I inferred from his broken sentence worse perhaps than he intended."

²⁷²*Con l'altro che...*: Italian for "with the other [words] that followed." *Inferno* IX, 11.

in questo fondo della trista conca.[273]

But Virgil then feigns to misunderstand the question?

Could be. Perhaps he wants Dante to be surprised by the auxiliary when he comes, and deludes the disciple. Yes, yes, I know the way: this bog lies somewhere around Dis. Something that Dante already figured out not long before:

> *Lo buon maestro disse: Omai, figliuolo,*
> *s'appressa la città che ha nome Dite,*
> *co' gravi cittadin, col grande suolo.*
>
> *Ed io: Maestro, già le sue meschite*
> *là entro certo nella valle cerno*
> *vermiglie, come se di foco uscite*
>
> *fossero...*
> *Noi pur giugnemmo dentro all'alte fosse,*
> *che vallan quella terra sconsolata:*
> *...*
> *Non senza prima far grande aggirata,*
> *venimmo in parte...*[274]

At another time, Virgil responds more or less

---

[273]*In questo fondo...*: Italian for "into this bottom of the sad basin."

[274]*Lo buon maestro disse...*: Italian for "The good master said: 'Now, son, the city called Dis draws near, with its grievous citizens, with its crowd.' And I: 'Master, already I discern some of its mosques there, vermillion as if they had just left the fire...' Then we reached deep moats that surround that disconsolate land:... Not without having first walked a long while around it, we came to a place... " *Inferno*, VII 67-80.

in this way; when Dante would like to know how far he has to go up the hill of Purgatory, that is, how high the hill is; then Virgil says: All I know is that when your going seems easy to you, you will be at the summit (*Purg.*, IV 85 ff). But also, if he did not want to accept this fiction, if he did not want it to be yet another instance of ingenious variety of the way in which the Master speaks to his disciple, it would always be acceptable for the Master to have understood his question as referring to the expected savior;

> ... *Di rado*
> *incontra, mi rispose, che di noi*
> *faccia il cammino alcun, pel quale io vado;*[275]

except that what follows, *to be honest*, signifies this: "in any case I can affirm to you that I have been here and that I know the way." Only, in this case Virgil does not seem to satisfy Dante; for the latter has no hope unless it is in the help provided by another, and he already has his doubts, and the former says that there is also something else, and that this can, without anyone else's help, guide him and allow him to enter into the grievous city. Only, for this to happen, *anger* is necessary.

At this point I might add to what the duke di Sermoneta said, my arguments being more than a reproof of his. One cannot enter without ANGER; heaven's messenger appears FULL OF DISDAIN, and speaks as such. He turns away then without saying a word, appearing to be

---

[275]*Di rado incontra*...: Italian for "'Rarely does it happen,' he said to me, 'for us to take the road that I am taking.'" *Inferno*, IX 19-21.

d'uomo cui altra cura stringa e morda,
che quella di colui che gli è davante.[276]

Are these three particulars idle? Listening to
the commentators, they would seem so. And yet they
have a profound meaning. The Poet speaks in symbols. He continues his admirable treatment of *anger*
or *irascibility*. Without this or that the difficult task is
inaccessible. Virgil first tries to enter with the good,
using his intellect:

Così sen va e quivi m'abbandona
lo dolce padre, ed io rimango in forse,
chè 'l sì e 'l no nel capo mi tenzona.

Udir non pote' quel ch'a lor si porse:
ma ei non stette là con essi guari,
che ciascun dentro a prova si ricorse.

Chiuser le porte que' nostri avversari
nel petto al mio signor, che fuor rimase,
e rivolsesi a me con passi rari.

Gli occhi alla terra e le ciglia avea rase
d'ogni baldanza, e dicea ne' sospiri:
chi m'ha negate le dolenti case?[277]

---

[276]*D'uomo cui altra cura...*: Italian for "a man whom other cares
worry and gnaw at more than what is before him." *Inferno*, IX
102-3.

[277]*Così sen va...*: Italian for "So he went away, and left me there,
the gentle father, and I remain in doubt, unsure what to do next. I
could not hear what he said to them; but he did not stay with
them for long, as each ran back as fast as he could. Those
adversaries of ours shut the door in my lord's face, who remained
without, and returned to me with unusual step. Eyes to the

Dante, ever focused on his philosophy, presents Virgil here as if tempted by acedia, by sadness, which is an acquiescence to evil. But it is just for a moment.

> *Ed a me disse: Tu, perch'io m'adiri,*
> *non sbigottir, ch'io vincerò la prova,*
> *qual ch'alla difension dentro s'aggiri.*[278]

Where it is to be noted that *because* does not mean exactly *nevertheless,* but *for the fact that;* and something else as well: that the second of my preceding interpretations of the response to Dante is the more likely, by which Virgil would promise Dante victory and passage, even if the messenger did not come.

Therefore, Dante is not afraid for the fact that Virgil must *be angry*; in other words, that he employs irascibility when faced with difficulty: righteous anger, without which he vilifies himself. There is no need for it however. In order to represent the necessary contemporaneity of irascibility, Dante [the poet] introduces the hero who has once already served as an example both to curb concupiscence and to spur irascibility. "This spurring was what was seen when Aeneas, *with only the Sibyl,* undertook entering Hell in

---

ground and face deprived of every self-confidence, and he said with sighs: 'They have denied me entrance into the house of the afflicted!'" *Inferno,* VIII 109-120.

[278]*Ed a me disse*...: Italian for "And he said to me: 'You, because I am *angry*, do not be dismayed, for in the end I will win, and whatever obstacle is in the way, you will get around it." *Inferno,* VIII 121-123.

order to search for the soul of his father Anchises
against *so many dangers*" (*Conv.*, IV 26). The singu-
lar correspondence of the phrase

> *passando per li cherchi senza scorta*[279]

with that of "*with only the Sibyl*" does not escape us.
As usual, there was no need to put into rhyme or fill
in the verse to explain what *senza scorta* suggested.
Nor is it to be forgotten that the phrase *contro a tanti
pericoli*[280] is suggested probably by those two passages in the sixth book *della detta storia*.[281]

The first are the words of the Sibyl:

> *Nunc animis opus, Aenea, nunc pectore*
> *firmo:*[282]

where *animi, pectus* are, for Dante, irascibility, θυμός,
or "heart." The other is:

> *Centauri in foribus stabulant Scyllaeque biformes*
> *Et centumgeminus Briareus ac belua Lernae*
> *Horrendum stidens flammisque armata Chimaera,*
> *Gorgones Harpyiaeque et forma tricorporis*
>   *umbrae.*
> *Corripit hic subita trepidus formidine ferrum*

---

[279]*Passando per...*: Italian for "passing through the circles without
an escort." *Inferno*, VIII 129.

[280]*Contro a tanti pericoli*: Italian for "against so many dangers."

[281]*Della detta storia*: Italian for "of the said story."

[282]*Nunc animis opus...*: Latin for "Now show your courage,
Aeneas, now your resolve." *Aeneid*, VI 261.

Aeneas strictamque aciem venientibus offert.[283]

The which passages were in front of the Poet, even at this point in the *Comedy*.

From these considerations, it is particularly confirmed (or I am mistaken) first that the messenger is Aeneas; second that the bog, which both the filthy souls with apparent offense and those thick in the mud cannot get out of, even though someone from the first group tries to climb into Phlegyas' boat, – that the bog contains those who sinned in irascibility or acquiesced in evil like the *sad* souls and probably the *great kings*, or did not go so far as to act on their superabundant irascibility, but turned on themselves instead, with their teeth, gnawing on themselves with anger and not sinning other than through self-directed anger, without resorting to vengeance; this also is acedia and sadness. And incidentally, with respect to the *great kings*, I am reminded of the 9th tale of the first day in the *Decameron.* Behold a king who, if not for the good fortune of a lady of Gascony, would have merited being like a *pig in filth.* The words of Boccaccio are noted: "*egli di cattivo, valoroso deviene*",[284] "*il re, infino allora stato* tardo e pigro."[285] These others should be considered: "*egli era di sì*

---

[283]*Centauri in foribus*...: Latin for "Centaurs, and double shapes, besiege the door. Before the passage, horrid Hydra stands, And Briareus with all his hundred hands; Gorgons, Geryon with his triple frame; And vain Chimaera vomits empty flame. The chief unsheath'd his shining steel, prepar'd." (John Dryden's translation.) *Aeneid*, VI 286-291.

[284]*Egli di cattivo*...: Italian for "from a bad man, he became a valient one." *Decameron*, First Day, Ninth Tale.

*rimessa vita e da sì poco bene, che, non che egli l'al-
trui onte con* giustizia *vendicasse, anzi infinite con vi-
tuperevole* viltà *a lui fattene sosteneva... io non vengo
nella tua presenza per vendetta che io attenda della*
ingiuria *che m'è stata fatta."*[286] Dante's concept is
well illustrated by this example. In the bog, cowardice
or lack of activity is punished, which has to be *justice*
for everyone involved, but especially for the kings,
negligentia in short, and the injustice that is not committed except by lack of activity. He passes through
the bog with dry feet, as if it were dry ground to him,
he who is supremely *active* and *just*, well adapted to
rein in or to spur his appetite. For Dante, the messenger was Aeneas, whom already in the first colloquy
Virgil called *just*:

> *... cantai di quel giusto
> figliuol d'Anchise;*[287]

which here means *active*, in addition to the action itself that he takes, those actions in which he shows
himself to be occupied:

> *... fe' sembiante*

---

[285]*Il re, infino...*: Italian for "the king, up until now lazy and
apathetic." ibid.

[286]*Egli era di sì rimessa vita...*: Italian for "so spiritless and
fainèant was he that he not only neglected to avenge affronts put
upon others, but endured with a reprehensible tameness those
that were offered to himself... 'it is not to seek redress of the
wrong done me that I come here before you.'" (J. M. Rigg's
translation) ibid.

[287]*Cantai di quel...*: Italian for "I sang of that just son of Anchise."
Inferno, I 73-74.

> *d'uomo cui altra cura stringa e morda*
> *che quella di colui che gli è davante;*[288]

Aeneas, his Master's hero, who served as an example to him since the *Convivio*.

II.
The Count Ugolino

I ask myself, together with a fine fellow, a shrewd critic if ever there was one, d'Ovidio[289]: for what reason the Count Ugolino was in Hell, in the ice? But I am not satisfied by his response, which is that he is damned for his betrayals against his nephew Ugolino Visconti. If that were true, why is he not in Caina? In Caina where Sassol Mascheroni is, murderer of a little cousin, where Camicion de' Pazzi is, murderer as well of a kinsman? In Caina, where those who broke the bond of love that joins people together are punished, not only children with respect to their parents, but parents in general with respect to relatives? Those, as it seems to have been demonstrated to me, who violated the fourth commandment?

To this objection, to tell the truth, I have one reply, and others will have a hundred; but I put forward mine, which, while it solves the problem contained in this matter, makes probable another, I don't

---

[288]*Fe' sembiante*...: Italian for "[he] had the look of a man whom other cares worry and gnaw at more than what is before him." *Inferno* IX, 101-3.

[289]Ovidio: Francesco D'Ovidio (AD 1849-1925), a philologist and critic of Italian literature.

say hypothesis, but conclusion. Because there will be, ultimately, a dispute between the two beliefs, the first one completely conjecturable, which has no support from Dante's work, and the other which has a very high likelihood based on Dante's work. It is true that others are placed in Hell or in the ice without the Poet saying why, while there had to be a reason and it was noted; and the same could be said for the Count Ugolino; but if the reason were to be found in a closer reading of the text? By a more reasonable interpretation?

Bartoli; dear and illustrious name, no longer alas! that name, a *large part* of him even; Bartoli finds in Ugolino's tale a suggestion of the crime of betrayal against Nino and against the Guelphs. He says (*Storia della letteratura italiana*, IV, part II, p. 111): "In the poem there is a phrase that confirms such supposition, that 'my trusting in him,' (v. 17), which otherwise, if there hadn't been an understanding between the count and the archbishop, would not have made sense. But trusting in Ubaldini necessarily implied being in strict league with a Ghibelline party and that could not be without harm to his nephew. Double betrayal therefore..." But I do not believe that *fidandomi di lui* is anything more than a reference to the definition of betrayal (*Inf.*, XI 52 ff):

> *La frode, ond'ogni coscienza è morsa,*
> *può l'uomo usare in colui che 'n lui fida.*[290]

---

[290]*La frode, ond'ogni...*: Italian for "Fraud, which gnaws away at every conscience, a man can use it against someone who trusts in him."

Dante makes Ugolino give the reason for the condemnation, not his but that of the archbishop's. He says: "You know the betrayal that he made against me, therefore you know why he is in this ice; what you don't know is how cruel the death was that I suffered on account of his betrayal, so you don't know why I am eating his head." Is this not the hint that Bartoli mentions then, which moreover is much more than a hint, which I claim is contained in the text, as to Ugolino's crime. O what is it then?

I will first address the objection made to Ovidio's position: given that Ugolino is not in Caina, did he break the bond that ties kinsman to kinsman or not? I respond: Ugolino is in Caina actually.

I hear an "*oh lungo e roco...*"[291] Let me explain. He is not in Caina, I repeat; but he *would* be if he were in his place. But in his place, which is where his crime would be punished, he is not. He is... Read this:

vidi due *ghiacciati in* una *buca;*[292]

where "una" has its numeral equivalency of "one," and not the indeterminate "a", in contradistinction to "two." The hole was made for one person only. So if two offenders are there, one of them is not in his proper place. Whoever thinks about it then, how in this ice there are offenders according to their mis-

---

[291]*Oh lungo e roco*: Italian for "a long and hoarse 'oh'." *Purgatory*, V 27.

[292]*Vidi due...*: Italian for "[Dante] saw *two* souls in *one* hole in the ice." *Inferno*, XXXII 125.

deed, not only located little by little toward the middle of it, but more or less sticking out of the ice, so that in Caina:

> *livide insin là dove appar vergogna*
> *eran l'ombre dolenti nella ghiaccia,*[293]

and in Antenora their faces can be seen, deformed because of the cold, where in passing Dante kicks with his foot into the *cheeks* of Bocca, and in Ptolomea the people are

> *non volta in giù ma tutta riversata,*[294]

and in Judecca

> *'l'ombre eran tutte coperte,*
> *e trasparean come festuca in vetro;*[295]

Whoever thinks about this gradation will see or, let me rephrase that, will suspect immediately that the two souls in one ice hole are not punished for the same crime at all, because

> *l'un capo all'altro era cappello.*[296]

---

[293]*Livide insin...*: Italian for "livid even there where the dolorous shades appear ashamed in the ice." *Inferno*, XXXII 34-35.

[294]*Non volta in giù...*: Italian for "not turned downward, but completely turned over." *Inferno*, XXXIII, 93.

[295]*L'ombre eran tutte...*: Italian for "the shades were all covered, and gleamed like straw in glass." *Inferno*, XXXIV 11-12.

[296]*L'un capo...*: Italian for "one's head served as another one's hat." *Inferno*, XXXII 126.

Which is not idle. Dante could have put these two sinners one after the other, like the two tragic Alberti brothers. But no. They were

> *... sì stretti*
> *che il pel del capo aveano insieme misto;*[297]

these, so close that the one's head was the other's hat:

> *sì che l'un capo all'altro era cappello.*

Dante has put us on guard, highlighting the difference in expressions that they have in similar between them: *pel del capo misto* and *capo cappello*.

Here's my take on it then: the Count Ugolino is not in his proper place in Antenora, because he is in a hole destined for another, where that other person is already. His having his head completely up out of the ice, so that it juts out with that of the other, makes us understand that he ought to be in Caina, where the offenders there stick out from the neck, so that they can butt heads like billygoats. And that is confirmed by another observation. The damned in the ice, in their quality as *proud* souls and for that reason supremely desirous in life for fame, are in death described by the Poet as fiercely averse to it. Thus Dante says to Bocca:

> *Vivo son io, e caro esser ti puote,*
> *fu mia risposta, se domandi fama*
> *ch'io metta il nome tuo tra l'altre note.*

---

[297]*Sì stretti che*...: Italian for "so close together that the hair of their heads were mixed together." *Inferno*, XXXII 42.

Ed egli a me: Del contrario ho io brama:
levati quinci and non mi dar più lagna,
chè mal sai lusingar per questa lama.[298]

Which is met again in the rest of the ice, and
particularly in Ptolomea, where Brother Alberigo
gives his name, but only because he thinks the two
visitors are cruel souls who have been assigned to the
last place. Now, not all the damned in the ice are really so contrary to identifying themselves or being identified; given that those of the first circuit identify
themselves, he identifies himself, that is, the only one
of them who speaks:

E perchè non mi metti in più sermoni,
sappi ch'io fui il Camicion de'i Pazzi,
ed aspetto Carlin che mi scagioni;[299]

and the two brothers prepare to identify themselves,
as they lift their faces, if it weren't for the fact that

gli occhi lor, ch'eran pria pur dentro molli,
gocciar su per le labbra, e il gelo strinse
le lagrime tra essi e riserrolli:

con legno legno mai spranga non cinse
forte così; ond'ei, comem due becchi,

---

[298]*Vivo son io...*: Italian for "'I am alive and can be useful to you,'
was my response, 'if you wish for fame, I can add your name to
my list.' And he to me: 'I desire just the opposite. Off with you
then and stop bothering me, in that you are bad at cajoling in this
swamp.'" *Inferno* XXXII, 91-96.

[299]*E perchè non...*: Italian for "and to avoid you letting me ramble
on, know that I was Camicion de' Pazzi, and I wait for Carlino to
exonerate me." *Inferno*, XXXII 67-69.

cozzaro insieme, tant'ira li vinse.[300]

Considering how atrocious are the crimes committed by the offenders [held] in Caina, remembering, for example, Sassol Mascheroni, the assassin of a boy, it can be difficult to explain this difference in loathing of fame between them and the offenders who lie more close to the middle, not more fierce than them, unless one disbelieves what I have just exposed: that Caina punishes a sin which is pride to be sure, but also borders on envy; a sin that is not against the universal principle of being, as are the other three, but against that particular; a sin that does not offend God directly, even though it offends whoever continues to hold God dear; a sin that goes against the fourth commandment, which is not in the first tablet although it is very near and similar to it. But of this I have spoken elsewhere. Here I observe that the Count Ugolino identifies himself immediately:

Tu dei saper ch'io fui Conte Ugolino.[301]

For what reason is he in Caina then, if not *principally* this one?

And we ask the question again: what was his offense? Certainly that of sin against kinsmen. Not *betrayal* against kinsmen? I would hesitate to say *be-*

---

[300]*Gli occhi lor,...*: Italian for "their eyes, which at first were soft within, welled up with tears, and the cold froze the tears and sealed them shut. No board to board was ever clamped so tight before; whereupon they butted heads like two rams, so overcome with rage were they." *Inferno*, XXXII 46-51.

[301]*Tu dei saper...*: Italian for "You must know that I was count Ugolino." *Inferno*, XXXIII 13.

trayal. According to Dante, *betrayal,* yes, but as-
suredly without the words *against kinsmen*. *To betray,* in Dante, is to forget the love

> *che fa natura, e quel ch'è poi aggiunto,*
> *di che la fede spezial si cria.*[302]

Now for the mode of *betrayal*, which is punished in Caina, one forgets that natural and additional
love, even if fraud or deception or ambush does not
figure into it, even if betrayal such as we conceive of
it is not involved. Francesca's husband, for having
killed his brother and his wife, is expected in Caina,
even if he was not the betrayer, the poor man!

And, in truth, even in the other three types of
fraud where trust is involved, it is not necessary that
fraud, as we understand it, be there; and Brutus and
Cassius are not therefore punished because they
caught Caesar by surprise in the curia, but because
they murdered him, because they violated God in the
act. Nonetheless, in these three types of fraud there is
always the breaking of a pact, not strictly the swear-
ing of an oath, a pact that does not always seem to us
so tacit and natural as it seemed to Dante for all and
sundry, and as it appears to us for the first time. Let
us say then that Ugolino's crime, while deserving of
Caina, is not necessarily the fraudulent offense of a
blood tie, but it is an offense clearly; which can be
said, more or less, of the other crimes punished in the
three internal circuits of the ice, but always less toward the exterior, especially considering the murder-

---

[302]*Che fa natura...*: Italian for "that nature makes, and in addition,
the special trust that is created." *Inferno*, XI 62-63.

ers of guests, always perjurers. It is not necessary, in fact it is not probable. Some aggravating circumstance of an ambush, a perjury, a violated guest, an abandoned party would have induced the Poet to place the count more *in ver lo mezzo*.[303]

It seems probable to me then that Ugolino's crime was an offense against a blood tie, independent of ambush. But here someone may say: The objection that you at first made to d'Ovidio, you did not need to make it or respond because, if Ugolino is in Antenora, it must be understood that he's there because he offended a relative, yes, but also because in addition to violating a familial bond, he violated the ties of his party or fatherland. No, I will say it again: he is in Antenora, but not of Antenora. However my reasoning might have begun, it is certain that the count belongs in Caina, for three firm arguments: his being in the *hole* of another, his sticking up his head, his giving his name without horror of fame. But with respect to this last argument, I anticipate a new opposition. It is this: even in Malebolge one has a horror of fame, in Malebolge where envy is punished, and that for the similarity that exists between envy and pride; whence similar effects derive; so that envy, coming from the fear of losing

> *podere, grazia, onore e fama,*[304]

just like pride, coming from the hope for excellence, both are punished with the hatred of that which gener-

---

[303]*In ver lo mezzo*: Italian for "toward the middle." *Inferno*, X 134.

[304]*Podere, grazia*...: Italian for "power, favor, honor and fame." *Purgatory*, XVII 118.

ates and nourishes them. Now, this new opposition does not really add anything other than the corroboration of what I affirm: that Caina punishes a sin [that lies somewhere] between pride and envy, because it has this characteristic in common with Malebolge that, just as in Malebolge, so too in Caina, the supposed rule that one does not give one's name admits exceptions, and it admits them for two reasons, both of which derive from envy being a sin against men, while pride is a sin against God. First reason: that the invidious show their desire to remain as they are, not pessimists; second, that the desire to do evil against their neighbor in them, not as stupid as the proud who raise their eyebrows at God, still persists, either underhandedly as in Capocchio and in Maestro Adamo, or ferociously as in Ugolino. This difference between the invidious and the proud is indicated, as I explained, by Antaeus, who, not having been with his brothers at high war, is not only unbound and speaks, but is sensitive to the incantation of fame. Besides, in the ice, Camicion de' Pazzi is typical for the first reason that we mentioned, he who exclaims:

> *Sappi ch'io fui il Camicion de' Pazzi*
> *ed aspetto Carlin che mi scagioni;*[305]

and for the second reason, Ugolino, who declares:

> *Ma se le mie parole esser den seme*
> *che frutti infamia al traditor ch'io rodo,*

---

[305] *Sappi ch'io...*: Italian for "[You should] know that I was Camicion de' Pazzi, and I wait for Carlino to exonerate me." *Inferno*, XXXII 67-69.

> *parlare e lagrimar vedrai insieme.*[306]

Now, in Maleboge these two types are en-
countered here and there. Those among them who
give their names or hint at them, then name or hint at
someone more guilty than themselves, in their view,
and do or say the worst that they can: Ciampolo
names Brother Gomita and Micheal Zanche; Catalano
Caifasso; Pier de Medicina predicts misfortune:

> *A messer Guido ed anco ad Angiolello,*[307]

Mosca hints at the worsening of the Tuscan
people; Bertram del Bornio recalls Achitofel; Capocchio, with the irony particular to the envious who
want to speak badly without appearing to, lists Stricca
and Niccolò and Caccia d'Asciano and Abbagliato;
and Griffolino reveals Gianni Schicchi and Myrrha.
Nor is the horrible fray of robbers to be forgotten, nor
is Maestro Adamo's indecent altercation with Sinone
to be left out, in which all Dante's thought about the
invidious of hell is epitomized. As for Vanni Fucci, I
have already said enough.

I conclude therefore, for the second time, that
the Count Ugolino is damned *to* Caina, if not *of*
Caina. What is the blood tie that he offended? Which
one? The one, I estimate, that the betrayer precisely
drove him to, whom he gnaws on in order to avenge

---

[306]*Ma se le parole*...: Italian for "But if my words must be the
seeds that produce infamy to the traitor I gnaw on, you will see
tears as I speak." *Inferno*, XXXIII 7-9.

[307]*A messer Guido*...: Italian for "to Messer Guido and also to
Angiolello." *Inferno*, XXVII 77.

himself. Because not of the *first* death, but of the *second,* is it reasonable for him to avenge himself, a damned person in hell. Whom does Pier della Vigna accuse and of what? He killed himself: his offense, and his injury! But no: Pier della Vigna accuses:

> *La meretrice che mai dall'ospizio*
> *di Cesare non torse gli occhi putti,*
> *morte comune e delle corti vizio,*
>
> *infiammò contra me gli animi tutti;*
> *e gl'infiammati infiammar sì Augusto*
> *che I lieti onor tornaro in tristi lutti.*
>
> *L'animo mio per disdegnoso gusto*
> *credendo col morir fuggir disdegno*
> *ingiusto fece me contra me giusto.*[308]

It was his mind or *heart,* irascibility that is, that drove him to suicide, but he had been led to it by the invidiousness of the court. Nor does he accuse them of his death, but of having made him unjust against himself; as if to say, of his own damnation. And he speaks, as someone who was unjust in that one act and under the goadings of θυμός, in a measured and equitable fashion, accusing *invidia* rather than the invidious, and affirming himself *worthy of honor,* he who had been the more direct cause of his

---

[308]*La meretrice che*...: Italian for "The whore, who never turned her whorish eyes away from Caesar's house, the death of all and the vice of the court, she inflamed all hearts against me, and those inflamed inflamed Augustus, so that agreeable honor turned into grievous mourning. My soul, by scornful pleasure, believing to escape that scorn through death, made me act unjustly against myself, the just." *Inferno,* 13 64-72.

death. But let us think about Guido di Montefeltro:

> *In fui uom d'arme, e poi fui cordigliero,*
> *credendomi, sì cinto, fare ammenda;*
> *e certo il creder mio veniva intero,*
>
> *se non fosse il gran prete, a cui mal prenda,*
> *che mi rimise nelle prime colpe:*
> *e come e quare voglio che m'intenda...*
>
> *... e pentuto e confesso mi rendei:*
> *ahi miser lasso! e giovato sarebbe.*
> *Lo principe de' nuovi farisei,*[309]

in what follows. He accuses, then, Boniface for his death; a spiritual, not a corporal death is meant: the *second*, not the *first*. Oh! Manfred does not accuse anyone, although he died with

> *... rotta la persona*
> *di due punte mortali,*[310]

for that is not a true death wherein one does not lose eternal love; indeed, he has an inspiration to reacquire it; not Buonconte, so that he could finish uttering the

---

[309]*Io fui uom d'arme...*: Italian for "I was a man of war, and then a friar, believing I could amend myself in robes, and I surely would have succeeded if it weren't for a great priest, who be damned! had me practicing my old ways; and how and *why* that happened, I wish to tell you... and I repented and confessed; ah! woe is me! and I would have been happy. The prince of new Pharisees..." *Inferno*, XXVII 67-72, 83-85.

[310]*Rotta la persona...*: Italian for "a body broken by two mortal wounds." *Purgatory*, III 118-9.

name of Mary;[311] not La Pia, whom Maremma did not undo so as to damn her gentle soul. La Pia does not accuse

> *...colui che inanellata pria,*
> *disposando, l'avea con la sua gemma,*[312]

just as Piccarda does not accuse the men who kidnapped her from the convent of being *mal più ch'a ben usi*[313], given that their efforts were in vain or almost in vain, and she chants an *Ave Maria* over it; but another, Francesca, although an offender, accuses and both grieves and imprecates:

> *Amor, che al cor gentil ratto s'apprende,*
> *prese costui della bella persona*
> *che mi fu tolta,* e il modo ancor m'offende,...
>
> *Amor condusse noi ad una morte:*
> *Caina attende chi vita ci spense.*[314]

Why does Francesca imprecate, or predict misfortune? Because her life which was extinguished

---

[311]*Not Buonconte...: Purgatory*, V 100-101.

[312]*Colui che inanellata...*: Italian for "he who proposed to me, slipping this gem on my finger." *Purgatory* V, 135-6.

[313]*Mal più ch'a ben usi*: Italian for "more used to ill than to good." *Paradise*, III 106.

[314]*Amor, che al cor...*: Italian for "Love, which quickly takes hold of the gentle heart, took hold of him for the beautiful person that was taken away from me; *and I'm still hurt by the way he did it...* Love brought us to our death. Caina awaits him who took our lives." *Inferno* V, 100-2, 106-7.

is not merely the temporal one, but the eternal one; because the beautiful person was taken away from her in a way that *still offends her*, that is, hers is an injury that will last forever, because it leaves no room for penitence. So that Dante calls them *offended,* those souls who were the victims of love, for *one reason only.* Now, doesn't Ugolino say that just like Francesca? Ugolino and Francesca weep while telling their stories, like someone who shares with others a large part of the guilt that they do not even disacknowledge.

> *Farò come colui che piange e dice,*[315]

sighs the one; and the other:

> *Parlar e lagrimar vedrai insieme.*[316]

Now, these sufferers clearly make known that they were harmed, the one saying

> *e il modo ancor m'offende;*

and the other exclaiming:

> *e vedrai se m'ha offeso.*

In what does Ugolino declare himself *offended?*

> *Però quel che non puoi avere inteso,*

---

[315]*Farò come colui che*...: Italian for "I will do like someone who weeps and speaks." *Inferno* V, 126.

[316]*Parlar e lagrimar*...: Italian for "you will see tears as I speak ." *Inferno* XXXIII, 9.

ciò è come la morte mia fu cruda,
udirai, e saprai se m'ha offeso.[317]

(come == quomodo).[318] Well do I know: everyone interprets it like this:

"You do not know the particulars of my death by starvation, it having come after that of my sons and nephews: therefore you do not know in what way I have the right to hate that betrayer." But to such an interpretation I oppose this one which appears to me more reasonable and more expressive in everything and for every reason:

"You cannot however have understood the way in which I died: only then will you know that he not only gave me a corporal death, but also a spiritual one: for it was the *way* he did it that *still hurts me*." The reader should step back for a moment from the meaning that it habitually possesses, more, one might say, in the ear than in the mind. Step back... and say whether it isn't almost ridiculous, that

saprai se m'ha offeso.

"Ah! you doubt whether I am right to complain about him? You may doubt it, but know, as you do, that I was betrayed by him, taken and killed – killed in the Muda, by starvation, with my sons" (this too Ugolino knows that Dante must know:

---

[317]*Però quel che...*: Italian for "But what you cannot have heard is in what way my death was cruel, you shall hear and you shall know whether he wronged me." *Inferno*, XXXIII 19-21.

[318]*(Come == quomodo)*: Italian for "(*come* == in what way)."

> *Breve pertugio dentro dalla muda*
> la qual per me ha il titol della fame;[319]

were notorious things, and as such, the count talks about them without preamble): "knowing merely this, you can doubt it: but can you doubt *that he harmed me*, when you know that I heard the sound of the boys crying; when Anselmuccio said to me: 'You look so, – father what is it?' that I bit my hand, and you were saying?" No no no: that the archbishop had offended Ugolino and in a most serious way, Dante already knew that, because he knew about his capture and his death in the Muda. To his question:

> *O tu che mostri per sì bestial segno*
> *odio sopra colui che tu ti mangi,*
> *dimmi il perchè, diss'io, per tal convegno*
>
> *che, se tu a ragion di lui ti piangi,*
> *sappiendo chi voi siete, e la sua pecca,*
> *nel mondo suso ancor io te ne cangi*
>
> *se quella con ch'io parlo non si secca;*[320]

to the words, *se tu a ragion di lui ti piangi*, he replied adequately with

---

[319]*Breve pertugio...*: Italian for "A narrow window in the Muda, the which tower that because of me has been nicknamed starvation." *Inferno* XXXIII, 22-23.

[320]*O tu che mostri...*: Italian for "'O you who show by so bestial a sign the hatred you have for him you eat, tell me why,' I said, 'by such agreement, that if you are right to complain about him, knowing who you are and what his sin is, in the world above I will still repay you for it, if that with which I speak is not dried up." *Inferno* 32, 133-139.

Tu dei saper che io fui conte Ugolino
e questi l'arcivescovo Ruggieri.[321]

Why does Ugolino continue with:

Or ti dirò perchè i son tal vicino,[322]

or, in other words, why – *me lo mangio*[323]? Because
Ugolino understood better than the commentators; he
understood rightly that he cannot mourn for his betrayer, the one dead for the other one who is also
dead, unless because of a wrong, an *offensione*
(*Purg.*, XVII 82) according to the meaning that Dante
appears to attribute to this verb *offendere e ledere* in
multiple places; an *offensione* and an injury that en-
dures however. And this injury is not death, but
much, much crueler, – that of dying while in a state of
sin.

Who can say to himself: Well, it is like this
and nobody can deny it, even if nobody affirms it.
The archbishop has wronged the count by making
him die so cruelly, and he didn't think to repent of his
sins or didn't despair of his eternal salvation... As you
can see, that is implausible *Dantesquely* speaking.
Dante was right; and a father, thus martyred, would
not have condemned him then in that way, any more
than a chronicler tells how this father yelled from the

---

[321]*Tu dei saper...*: Italian for "You must know that I was count
Ugolino and this is the archbishop Ruggieri." *Inferno*, XXXIII 13-4.

[322]*Or ti dirò...*: Italian for "Now I will tell you why I am such a one's
neighbor." *Inferno*, XXXIII 15.

[323]*Me lo mangio*: Italian for "do I devour him."

Muda: "Penance! penance!" And there is something else. Dante, like the traveler through so strange a land, reports things on his return that he would not have known if he had not gone on such a trip. He satisfies, or tries to satisfy, insatiable curiosity, solving unsolvable problems. Where did Buonconte go at death? What happened to La Pia? Manfred died repentant or in contumacy? And in our case, the Count Ugolino... Yes; anyone could ask in what order he and his sons and nephews died, what words were spoken, what feelings felt, what dreams, what terrors, what anguishments, what torments; but in those days one needed to ask about everyone from a survivor of the world of the dead, and as with Manfred so with La Pia, as with Buonconte so with Ugolino: did they repent? are they in a state of salvation? Now, as for Manfred or Bounconte or La Pia, nobody knew anything about them, whether they had repented or not, and everyone, two of them at least, had to lean toward believing they hadn't; as for Ugolino, about whom it was affirmed that, yes, he had asked for penance, and he died in the presence of his sons who died before him, Dante would have responded: "Naturally, he is in hell, for betrayal, not for having betrayed Pisa *of the castles* however, but for another betrayal, which is not important to mention"? That repugns. But he is a poet, one might add; and the drama of the two souls in the one hole, where the one gnaws on the head of the other, must have particularly delighted him, delighted him more than justice. Indeed: just those two beings in one hole, and that one eating the other, if anything; while he could have put the story of Ugolino in Purgatory, with that of Manfred, with that of

Buonconte; even in Paradise, I was about to say... Is it possible to believe that that particular taken from Statius was worth, in Dante's soul, making him forget compassion, which he demonstrates so much of however, for the most unhappy father?

But let us conclude. It seems likely that Ugolino is in the ice on account of a sin that he committed there in the Muda, in death, in relation to the cruelty of that death. What? Dante hints at it when he says – *colui che tu ti mangi*. Ugolino says he gnaws, but Dante says *he devours*. Tydeus gnawed on Menalippus' temples, but Ugolino worked *on the skull and other things*. Dante hints at it even more with the loud cracking of the bones under the teeth of a dog, by which action the damned soul emphasizes and comments on the mysterious verse:

Poscia più che il dolor potè il digiuno.[324]

The father and grandfather violated with his teeth the flesh, perhaps the skull, of some of his sons and nephews. Was it true? There is no record of it; but Dante could have been made to believe it, whether it was true or not. Or he could have imagined it or invented it. And would that have been worthy of the just poet? It would not have been unworthy; because justice for him means to show that whoever committed a sin was punished and whoever repented and did good was rewarded; he does not really pretend to be believed with respect to crime and its punishment, good deeds and their reward, and especially

---

[324]*Poscia più che...*: Italian for "then hunger overcame mourning." Inferno, XXXIII 75.

in certain particulars, which clearly he invents, like Manfred's conversion and Buonconte's death and Ugolino's savage last meal. But to invent things contrary to known truths? For there are those who say they saw the cadavers and saw them without signs that would have raised suspicion. But one would need to prove that Dante knew about such recognition, or instead that he had uncertain information about the Pisan tragedy, as is perceived in this passage by Bargigi: "they practiced savage cruelty by letting them die in captivity: *it is thought to be certain that they died of starvation*." And in another place there is this, by way of comparison, by a Pisan chronicler: "the other three died that same week; *also* by starvation, because they do not pay." And that Dante did not know the actual drama in all its particular details can be seen by the fact that he calls all four captives the *sons* of the deceased count, and has Anselmuccio call him *father*, and says that Gaddo and Uguccione are of *a tender age*, so as to make them *innocents.* If he invented, it is quite clear that he had an open field to invent in, I will put it like that, he was free to invent, as he did with Buonconte and Manfred, and did not expect to be believed; but Dante wanted for the last episode of his hell, after so many other awful, horrid, atrocious stories, the most awful, horrendous, atrocious story of all.

But the episode is not beautiful like that! So many beautiful observations that want, here to prop up Dante's poetry, there to plaster over it, crumble to pieces and fall over! Gently now. Put it to the test. I do not want to repeat here someone else's right and fine observations, specially those by Antonio Dall'Acqua Giusti, nor do I try to reconstruct here the drama, which much more effectively succeeds with so many more reasonable interpretations. Here I content myself with some hint.

Consider this passage:

> ... *Ed Anselmuccio mio*
> *disse: Tu guardi sì, padre, che hai?*[325]

When the father became *blind*, what did he do to that poor Anselmuccio?

> *Ed ei, pensando ch'io il fessi per voglia*
> *di manicar, di subito levorsi,*
> *e disser: Padre...*[326]

alas, they thought only of him, they offered themselves to him like a meal; and he... afterwards... when he was blind...

> *Ahi, dura terra perchè non t'apristi?*[327]

whereupon, if not to prevent the horrible deed, the extremely nefarious acceptance of their most pious offer? But here is the most *ineffable* and tragic thought:

---

[325]*Ed Anselmuccio mio*...: Italian for "And my little Anselmuccio said: 'You look so, – Father, what is it?'" *Inferno*, XXXIII 50-1.

[326]*Ed ei, pensando*...: Italian for "And he, thinking that I did it because of hunger, immediately rose and said: Father..." *Inferno*, XXXIII 59-61.

[327]*Ahi, dura terra*...: Italian for "Ah, hard earth, why did you not open up?" *Inferno*, XXXIII 66.

due dì li chiamai...[328]

Nobody believes that he... Oh! no: it is un-speakable. They were *dead*, you understand? *They were no longer alive*, not even a little, not so much as a feeling... that intense activity of the teeth, that gnawing, that biting. And he who groped over them, the *father, was already blind*... His hunger was furi-ous. Oh! the sounds of it at this point, full and round, of him letting his teeth find their way and gnash through the skull bones! How just the imprecation of the *renewed Thebes* that bursts out! Renewed Thebes, because it made Ugolino repeat that Tydeus, *effracti perfusum tabe cerebri,* and *vivo scelerantem san-guine fauces* (*Thebaid.*, VIII 761 ff).[329] No other per-son was in the mind of the poet, who begins the tale precisely with his recollection of Tydeus, and finishes it with that exclamation, in which the words "*Poichè i vicini...*"[330] etc. are derived from the beginning of book IX of the *Thebaid*: *Asperat Aonios rabies audita cruenti Tydeos*;[331] and others – like "*che se il con-te...*"[332] – seem like a comment on Statius' strong ex-

---

[328]*Due dì li chiamai...*: Italian for "for two days, I called them." *Inferno*, XXXIII 74.

[329]*Effracti perfusum...*: Latin for "drenched in the putrefaction of smashed brains" and "polluted by the warm blood in his mouth." *Thebaid,* VIII 760. The *Thebaid,* an epic poem by Roman poet Publius Papinius Statius (AD 45-96).

[330]*Poichè i vicini...*: Italian for "because your neighbors..." *Inferno*, XXXIII 81.

[331]*Asperat Aonios...*: Latin for "News of Tydeus' cruel fury exasperated the Aonians." *Thebaid* IX, 1-2.

pression, *rupisse fas odii.*[333] Also, to conclude, there is in Statius an expression that alone can inform us what might be the meaning of a line of verse by Dante:

> ... *io scorsi*
> *per quattro visi il mio aspetto stesso.*[334]

Statius recounts:

> *Erigitur Tydeus vultuque occurrit et amens*
> *Laetitiaque iraque, ut singultantia vidit*
> *Ora trahique oculos,* seseque agnovit in ille*;*
> *Imperat abscisum porgi...*[335]

Tydeus, on seeing *his death* in the face of his attacker, conceives of his atrocious act: he has that head cut off, has it handed to him, gnaws on it, eats it. Ugolino... bites his own hands, but *out of anger*, for the time being. Moreover, by that gesture his sons predict; by the sons' words that in that gesture they had seen the desire to chow down (they had seen it in his eyes in a flash because

---

[332]*Che se il conte*...: Italian for "that if the count." *Inferno*, XXXIII 85.

[333]*Rupisse fas odii:* Latin for "to have broken the sacred bounds of hatred." *Thebaid* IX, 3-4.

[334]*Io scorsi*...: Italian for "I caught a glimpse of my own expression in their four faces." *Inferno*, XXXIII 56-7.

[335]*Erigitur Tydeus vultuque*...: Latin for "Tydeus rose and, mad with joy and anger, looked at him and saw his gasping face, and recognized his work in it, and ordered them to cut off his head, and he took it in his left hand." *Thebaid* VIII, 760-3.

di subito levorsi;)[336]

the miserable man, perhaps he anticipated the feral, indeed the *canine,* conclusion to the tragedy.

Oh! whoever has wept already for the last episode in the *Inferno*, as he wept for the first (the two lovers, the two enemies: how similar they seem!), has not wept enough if he did not interpret it as I interpret it. Look at one's children, if you are a father: and think how Dante dared to imagine and to represent a father reduced to such an enormous and infamous desperation of sinking his teeth into the skull of them, of them, of them!

III.
Bartoli's and Other Commentators and Critics' Difficulty

1.

Let's take up the sixth tome of the history of Italian literature by Bartoli, and from this tome the first part, where it is summarized and judged what constituted the thought up until that time (1887) on the fundamental conception of the *D.C.* and on the moral construction of the three realms. Let's focus on the points on which the illustrious critic focuses his attention and has his doubts, and let's see whether, after my study, there is any more reason to doubt.

Missing, unfortunately, is the subtle genius

---

[336]*Di subito levorsi*: Italian for "immediately he stood up." *Inferno,* XXXIII 60.

who would have shown greater judgment; the noble heart that more faithfully would have recognized the truth and untruths of this research!

From pp. 36-37:

The conception of the Divine Comedy *is without a doubt ethico-religious; the execution is in large part political. We follow rapidly behind this man who from the forest of vice wants to climb the mountain of Christian perfection. Among the first damned that he encounters are those of lust; but not a single word of abomination leaves his lips when he speaks with two among them: just the opposite: he almost seems to envy the happiness of their love, when, after the story of Francesca, Virgil asks: "What do you think?" and he responds:*

> Quanti dolci pensier, quanto disio
> Menò costoro al doloroso passo![337]

And not satisfied with that, he wants to know, he is curious to know, the whole drama of that unfortunate passion, and he asks:

> Ma dimmi, al tempo de' dolci sospiri,
> A che e come concedette Amore
> Che conosceste i dubbiosi disiri?[338]

---

[337] *Quanti dolci pensier...*: Italian for "Such sweet thoughts, so much desire led them to the dolorous pass." *Inferno*, V 113-114.

> *Is this the propagandist of truth and morality speaking, or the man, the old man who perhaps remembered his own loves, who perhaps was rethinking desirously about his own* sweet sighs?

O gentle soul, both the man and the poet are speaking here, but it is no less the philosopher or the theologian who expresses, without knitting his brow, his theological and philosophical truths. For Dante, there are the lustful, guilty simply of *incontinence*, and others guilty of *malice* or injustice, whom he wants to speak about. Francesca and Dido, Semiramis and Cleopatra, are among the first; Brunetto and Jason and Myrrha among the second. But Francesca is an adulteress, Semiramis incestuous, Dido and Cleopatra suicides... Yes, but for Dante it was their incontinence that caused those other problems; it was not the love of evil that produced such effects or instruments of incontinence. He says it clearly. Semiramis

> *A vizio di lussuria fu sì rotta*
> *Che libito fe' licito in sua legge,*
> *Per torre il biasmo, in che era condotta.*[339]

---

[338] *Ma dimmi, al tempo*...: Italian for "But tell me, at that time of sweet sighs, how and why you admitted Love and recognized your dubious desires." *Inferno*, V 118-120.

[339]*A vizio di lussuria*...: Italian for "was so hardened to the vice of lust, that she made it licit by law, to remove any wrong she had done." *Inferno*, V 55-7.

It was, therefore, the vice of lust, incontinence, *causa mali tanti*.[340] And Dido

> ... *s'ancise*[341]

yes, but

> *amororsa*,[342]

and Cleopatra is said to be not otiosely *lustful*.
Brunetto, on the other hand, wishes evil, rebelling
against God who had said, *Multiply*,[343] and impeding
for his own part the generation of progeny; and Jason
deceived Hypsipyle, and the wicked Myrrha concealed her identity; hence they are punished, the one
as guilty of anger against a good God, that is as a
stupid desirer of vengeance against his justice; the
second and third as guilty of envy, that is hypocrites
and hidden desirers and artificers of evil towards their
neighbor. But Francesca, oh! Dante lingers there in
that beautiful passage, to declare her guilty only of
immoderate love for a good which is not really good.
It was *Amor, che al cor gentil ratto s'apprende*,[344] it
was *Amor, che a nullo amato amar perdona*,[345] it was
Amor that led her and him to *their death*. They had

---

[340] *Causa mali tanti*: Italian for "the cause of so many evils."

[341] *S'ancise*: Italian for "killed herself." *Inferno*, V 61.

[342] *Amorosa*: Italian for "in love." ibid.

[343] Multiply: presumably in reference to Genesis 9:7, "be ye
fruitful, and multiply."

[344] *Amor, che al cor...*: Italian for "Love, which quickly takes hold of
the gentle heart." *Inferno*, V 100.

gentle thoughts, it was *desire,* it was *one thing only* that *overcame* them. Let's think about that: *one thing only!*

Let us say also that in his appraisal of the deed he is reminded of his own loves and thinks back with fondness on his own *dolci sospiri*; but let us add that once he had appraised it as a consequence of love, in other words incontinence, he was obliged by his fiction itself, by his philosophy and theology, not to show for those offenses, which they suffer for, even there, and make signs melancholically to God and in prayer, the abomination that was to grow gradually with each successive circle in hell, until the malediction made to Bocca, until the rudeness made to Brother Alberigo. Incontinence offends God less, says Virgil theoretically; and already Dante demonstrates it beforehand in fact. And, on the subject of lust, both that which is a conquest of love, as in the case of Francesca and Dido, and that which is an impiety of lust, as in the case of Semiramis, hardened to the vice of lust, and as in the case of the lustful Cleopatra. Because the people castigated in the dark atmosphere of Hell really seem to be of two minds: those hardened to vice, and those conquered by a desire. Semiramis leads the first group:

> *La prima di color di cui novelle*
> *Tu vuoi saper...;[346]*

---

[345]*Amor, che a nullo...*: Italian for "Love, which releases no lover from loving." *Inferno,* V 103.

[346]*La prima di color...*: Italian for "The first of those whose news you wish to know..." *Inferno,* V 52-3.

Dido is in the second group:

... *La schiera ov'è Dido.*[347]

And perhaps the first group is similar to the large and disordered flock of starlings, and the other to the long line of cranes that go *cantando lor lai*,[348] and to doves; but the souls of both one and the other are depicted as rapt by a force greater than themselves, *portate* (v. 49), and *gli stornei ne portan l'ali*[349] (*l'ali,* subject: v. 40) and the *colombe dal disio chiamate... vengon per l'aer... portate...*[350] yes, perhaps by their will, but even more so, perhaps even more so, by flight (cf. *fertur in arva volans*;[351] *Aeneid*, V 215; *illam fert impetus ipse volantem*, ib. 219[352]). There is even a difference between the ones and the others. What is it? This:

> *Nulla speranza gli conforta mai,*
> *Non che di posa, ma di minor pena.*[353]

Because two of the crowd that Dido is a part

---

[347]*La schiera ov'è Dido*: Italian for "The group where Dido is." *Inferno*, V 85.

[348]*Cantando lor lai*: Italian for "singing their lay." *Inferno*, V 46.

[349]*Li stornei...*: Italian for "the wings of the starlings carry them." *Inferno*, V 40.

[350]*Colombe dal disio...*: Italian for "the doves called by desire... borne through the air, come..." *Inferno*, V 82-4.

[351]*Fertur in arva volans*: Latin for "borne flying into the fields."

[352]*Illam fert impetus...*: Latin for "the impetus itself maintains that flight." *Aeneid*, V 219.

of have a moment of truce,

> *mentre che il vento, come fa, si tace;*[354]

it must be understood that the desperation of resting
and of minor punishment is proper only for sinners
similar to starlings, that is lechers, those hardened to
vice, those whom Semiramis stands out in front of.
And it is quite natural that only the others, those taken
and conquered by love, those whom *amor... mena,*
that they obey the incantation of love expressed by
the affectionate cry: *O anime affannate!*[355]

2.

And we move on to something else. Let's continue
reading:

> Pp. 37-38:
>
> *The same can be said about the fa-
> mous scene with Filippo Argenti. That
> if Dante here shouted at him:*
>
> > ... con piangere e con lutto
> > Spirito maledetto ti rimani,[356]
>
> *and if he is embraced and kissed by*

---

[353]*Nulla speranza gli conforta...*: Italian for "No hope ever
comforts them, not of rest, but of minor punishment." *Inferno*, V
44-5.

[354]*Mentre che il vento...*: Italian for "While the wind remains silent
as it does now." *Inferno*, V 82-4.

[355]*O anime affanate:* Italian for "O troubled souls!" *Inferno*, V 80.

Virgil and is called a 'scornful soul,'
we cannot yet suppose that all that ex-
presses the Poet's repulsion for the sin
that Argenti is punished for, but we
must believe by necessity either that
Dante had personal reasons, unknown
to us, to hate that [soul] 'filled with
filth'; or instead, as someone else has
supposed, in 'bizarre Florentine
mood,' that 'he turned on himself with
his teeth,' when he had wanted to rep-
resent the discord and Florentine citi-
zenry quarreling with itself. In any
case, he is always mindful of the world
above as he travels amongst the dead.

O gentle soul, with whom it is sweet for me to converse, our being separated not so much by land or sky or sea, but by life itself; it can be that Dante had personal reasons for hating that [soul] "filled with filth" and also that he wanted to represent the Florentine citizenry in him. But what is certain is that Dante wanted to represent in himself the man who repulses evil or the wicked, that he has in his irascibility the strength to *repel harm*, to hate *injustice* even when he showed himself by a refusal of justice, even when he did no harm, but turned on himself with his teeth. Crossing the bog of wicked slothfulness by boat (Dante is not Aeneas, the perfectly inured, who walks with dry soles; Aeneas to whom the Sibyl says: *invade viam vaginaque eripe ferrum; Nunc animis opus*

---

[356] *Con piangere e con lutto...*: Italian for "With weeping and with grieving, you remain an accursed spirit." *Inferno*, VIII 37-8.

Aenea, nunc pectore firmo![357]), he gives a display of himself as someone *d'alma sdegnosa*,[358] that is someone who has, with justice in mind, what those thick in the mud and others with offended countenances either did not have or had too much of, with consimilar effect of inactivity; that he has, in summary, irascibility. And he demonstrates having profited by the instruction that Virgil had given him before the absolutely slothful, before those who, not one amongst them, made a choice between good and evil. Virgil had told him then:

> *Misericordia e Giustizia li sdegna.*
> *Non ragioniam di lor, ma guarda e passa.*[359]

He had no need to bother with them, nor with those whom, deprived of the will of concupiscence and irascibility, the world did not let be *famous*; those of the bog, among whom are, or must come, the great kings who leave behind not only oblivion but contempt, among whom there is a *persona orgogliosa*,[360] a strong and good *maschera*, whose goodness is not what comes first to mind, – he must curse them and

---

[357]*Invade viam vaginaque*...: Latin for "On your way, and unsheathe your sword: Now show your courage, Aeneas, now your resolve." *Aeneid*, VI, 260-1.

[358]*D'alma sdegnosa*: Italian for "with an indignant soul." *Inferno*, VIII 44.

[359]*Misericoridia e Guistizia*...: Italian for "Compassion and Justice disdain them: let's not think about them, but look and move on." *Inferno*, III 50-1.

[360]*Persona orgogliosa*: Italian for "A proud person." *Inferno*, VIII 46.

reject them: *Spirito maledetto!* And the Poet concludes the episode with words that remind one of that
Non ragioniamo by Virgil: Let us leave him there,
chè più non ne narro.[361] The Poet's intention, not just
with respect to Argenti, but in the entire episode of
the bog up to the entrance into Dis, is to show besides
incontinence of irascibility and besides its defect, his
just temperament.

And he demonstrated it in himself, in Virgil,
and in Aeneas, completely.

As the slothful on the other side of the
Acheron are depicted by the Poet as condemned to a
vain and dolorous activity, running around perpetually and suffering from the stings of flies and wasps,
and crying; as these are depicted *invidiosi d'ogni altra sorte,*[362] not only of Paradise, which scornful Mercy forbids them; but also of Hell, where scornful Justice keeps them in the vestibule; thus the slothful of
evil, the incontinent of irascibility, are represented not
only as quarrelsome and seemingly offended and sad,
but also as having chosen *another destiny,* even the
worst punishments in Dis. But Justice too is contemptuous of them! *Via di qua con gli altri cani!*[363] Because Argenti evidently would like to move away
from that place, and he extends his hands to the boat
in order to climb in and make the crossing. *Vedi che*

---

[361]*Chè più non ne narro*: Italian for "whom I will not say anymore
about." Inferno, VIII 64.

[362]*Invidiosi d'ogni...*: Italian for "invidious of every other destiny."

[363]*Via di qua...*: Italian for "Off with you, with the other dogs."
Inferno, VIII 42.

son un che piango![364] he had said, as Palinurus [in the *Aeneid*] calls himself wretched, begging Aeneas:

> *Da dextram misero et tecum me tolle per undas!*[365]

And in the act and in the words of Virgil live, with natural transformation, the solemn warning of the Sibyl:

> *Unde haec, o Palinure, tibi tam dira cupido?*
> *...*
> *Desine fata deum flecti sperare precando.*[366]

3.

And we move on again to another passage, and precisely to the moral construction of the three Realms, the argument that forms Chapter II of the cited volume by A. Bartoli.

> Pp. 48-49:

> *... why, if they suffer eternally as one suffers in Hell, pull them (the wretched souls who never were alive) out of it? – Exactly – says Todeschini – this*

---

[364]*Vedi che son...*: Italian for "As you see, I am one who weeps." Inferno VIII 36.

[365]*Da dextram misero...*: Latin for "Reach out a hand! and carry me with you over the sea!" (*Aeneid,* VI 370).

[366]*Unde haec... precando*: Latin for "Whence this ominous desire, Palinurus?... Do not hope to deflect the fate of gods by praying." *Aeneid*, VI 373, 376.

dissonance between appearance and reality gives us the right to pick up again the instruction that was followed by the Poet. No one will grumble that Dante had placed a vestibule before the nine circles of Hell, but this laudable idea had to lead him to place the Limbo of the suspended elsewhere than there. – In the moral construction of the Inferno, this is without a doubt an error, or at least, as was said by Tomaseo – an insufficiently theological judgment. – But it is an error, however, even though it has its reasons, its lofty reasons, in the disdainful soul of the Poet.

It is an error, if one wishes, but one that has in truth its reasons, lofty or not, not so much in the disdainful soul of the Poet as in the design that he already delineated before touching the sacred poem. The slothful, who were never alive, are not only outside Hell, but on the farther side of the Acheron, while the suspended are not only within it, but on the nearer side. Why? Because even those of the fertile bog are outside the gates of Dis, and those that kill the soul together with the body are on the inside.

Now, the slothful and the filthy are apathetic, in diverse grades, but both with respect to an active life; the unbaptized and the heresiarchs are apathetic, in diverse grades, but both with respect to the contemplative life. Given the contemplative life is more worthy than the active, the lack of it in the first group is a greater error than in the second. Dante who is, besides a theologian, a man, corrects for his part that which in the practical application of this just principle vexed him as much as it offends us, adding the wasps and the big insects to the slothful on the outside, removing every martyr from the group of unbaptized within, making a noble castle for great spirits, throwing miserably into the mud the apathetic of evil, elevating with the figure of Farinata and with him if not the memory of great souls, such as Frederick II and the Cardinal, all the souls buried in the burning sepulchers, and principally representing those who are on the outside, those who are excluded by the Acheron and by Dis, as desirous to pass within, but in vain.

Now, the difficulties multiply. My responses follow step by step.

Page 50:

> ... *the first crimes punished are those of incontinence. In the second circle, the lustful, in the third the gluttonous, in the fourth the greedy and the prodigal, in the fifth the angry.*

Not precisely "the angry," but the incontinent of irascibility, those "who were conquered by anger" and those who were "sad," those who, to use the words from the *Convivio* (IV 26), were not *temperate* or *strong*, who did not apply either *restraint* or *spurs* to their appetite; brought together in the same bog, although in punishment and diverse attitudes; like the avaricious and the prodigal in the fourth circle. Vanquished by anger and sad therefore; but not guilty for the anger that was consummated, so to speak; in that they did not cause harm unless to themselves, or they tolerated harm done to themselves or to others. And they are all the *apathetic,* by lack of activity.

Which is completely natural to say about those thick in the mud (and it is indubitable, according to the passage by Gregorio Nysseno, *Accidia est tristitia quaedam vocem amputans*,[367] which I found by myself in the *Summa* and which afterwards I found in the *Commento* by Tommaseo, which no recent commentator, that I know of, drew from), but it can seem rather strange, given those who are quarrelsome, given those overcome by anger. Oh! would that it did not seem so! The anger *obstructed* them from acting, according to a procedure that the Poet describes in the Minotaur, which is the very symbol of anger:

> *quando vide noi, sè stesso morse*[368]

(as Argenti turned his teeth on himself),

> *sì come quei cui l'ira dentro fiacca,*[369]

which takes away, that is, their strength to act. From

---

[367]*Acedia est tristitia*...: Latin for "Acedia is a kind of sadness that cuts off the voice."

[368]*Quando vide noi*...: Italian for "When he saw us, he bit himself." *Inferno*, XII 14.

[369]*Sì come quei*...: Italian for "Just like those whose anger destroys within." *Inferno*, XII 15.

which, one easily understands how these whom irascibility dominated, while they needed to dominate it
with the reins of temperance, were however inactive
and apathetic like others who did not rouse the same
irascibility with the spur of fortitude. The effect of
such anger is mentioned in the *Summa* (1st of the 2nd,
XLVIII 2, 3, 4): *Ira maxime facit perturbationem
[corporalem] circa cor... ita ut etiam ad exteriora
membra derivetur.*[370] And a state of soul is common
to acedia and anger: *tristitia. Motus irae insurgit ex
aliqua illata iniuria contristante, cui quidem tristitiae
remedium adhibetur per vindictam*[371] (*Summa*, 1st of
the 2nd, XLVIII 1). It is clear that if vengeance is not
exacted, what remains is *tristitia*. Now Dante gets out
of it, and does not consider them offenders of anger
proper unless they exact vengeance: the others, incontinent of anger naturally but who did not exact
vengeance, he unites with the apathetic.

4.

Page 50:

> *From this it appears that Dante had
> differentiated the sinners in the circles
> of the* Inferno, *as with those in the cir-
> cles of* Purgatory, *according to the or-*

---

[370]*Ira maxime facit...*: Latin for "Great anger caused [bodily]
perturbation around the heart... which even affects the exterior
members."

[371]*Motus irae insurgit...*: Latin for "The movement of anger arises
from some received injury which causes sadness, for which
sadness a remedy is sought by way of vengeance."

der of mortal sins, but, naturally, in reverse order...

Excellent.

Page 51:

But having arrived at the sixth circle, there is a change.

Given the system in the *Inferno* had changed at this point, how ever would Dante have picked it up again then, entirely and perfectly, in *Purgatory*?

Page 51:

Mortal sins are no longer talked about, and instead the offenses are divided according to an entirely different concept, which the poet believes he needs to give an account of, and he does so in verses 70-83 of canto XI; verses from which he appears to have followed Aristotle's division, who in his Ethics *to Nicomachus (book VII c. I), says that there are three categories of thing that as far as morals are concerned are to be avoided: incontinence, vice, and bestiality.*

But having said that the offenses punished in the second, third, fourth, fifth circles are that of incontinence does not prevent these offenses from be-

ing declared lust, gluttony, avarice, and subjugation to
ire and sadness (let us call them that, but they are acedia); why not believe that the other two Aristotelian
divisions contain the other three mortal sins? All the
more so as Dante makes precisely three distinctions,
no more no less, of the other offenses which are reduced to bestiality and malice; that is, violence, fraud
in which there is no trust, fraud in which there is trust
or betrayal. Three and no more, like the sins that are
missing. O, is that not something to make one think?
But wait. Even in the treatment of offenses in *Purgatory* there is a definition and philosophical denomina-
tion of certain sins already referred to by their names
of sin. It is said (XVII 112 ff):

> *Resta, se dividendo bene estimo,*
> *che il mal che s'ama è del prossimo, ed esso*
> *amor nasce in tre modi in vostro limo.*
>
> *È chi, per esser suo vicin soppresso,*
> *spera eccellenza, e sol per questo brama*
> *ch'el sia di sua grandezza in basso messo;*
>
> *è chi podere, grazia, onore e fama*
> *teme di perder perch'altri sormonti,*
> *onde s'attrista sì, che il contrario ama;*
>
> *ed è chi per ingiuria par ch'adonti*
> *sì, che si fa della vendetta ghiotto;*
> *e tal convien che il male altrui impronti.*
>
> *Questo triforme amor quaggiù di sotto*
> *si piange.*[372]

---

[372]*Resta, se dividendo...*: Italian for "Hence if, discriminating, I

This triform love is reduced therefore to pride, envy and anger, with these names referred to as time goes on (*superbi cristian*, X 121; *la cervice mia superba*, XI 53; *superbia*, ib. 68; *di tal superbia*, ib. 88; *or superbite*, XII 70; *la copa della invidia*, ib. 135; *d'invidia*, XIV 82; *invidia*, XV 51; *in foco d'ira*, ib. 106; *d'iracondia*, XVI 24; *per ira*, XVII 36; *senza ira mala*, ib. 69).[373]

As for acedia, it is spoken of as follows (XVII 82 ff):

> *Dolce mio padre, dì quale offensione*
> *Si purga qui nel giro, dove semo?*
> *Se i pie' si stanno, non stea tuo sermone.*

> *Ed egli a me: l'amor del bene, scemo*
> *Di suo dover, quiritta si ristora,*
> *Qui si ribatte il mal tardato remo:*

> *Ma perchè più aperto intendi ancora...*[374]

Virgil begins the exposition of love as the ori-

___

judge well, the evil that one loves is of one's neighbour, and this is born in three modes in your clay. There are, who, by abasement of their neighbour, hope to excel, and therefore only long that from his greatness he may be cast down; there are [those] who power, grace, honour, and renown fear they may lose because another rises, thence are so sad that the reverse they love; and there are those whom injury seems to chafe, so that it makes them greedy for revenge, and such must needs shape out another's harm. this threefold love is wept for down below." (Longfellow's translation.) *Purgatory*, XVII 112-25.

[373] *Suberbia... invidia... ira/iraconda...*: Italian for "pride, envy, anger."

gin of every act of good and evil;

> *Se lento amore in lui veder vi tira,*
> *O a lui acquistar, questa cornice*
> *Dopo giusto penter, ve ne martira.*[375]

Virgil responded to his disciple's question in this way: "Which offense is atoned for in the ring where we find ourselves now?" And the disciple will understand better by the words (XVIII 107):

> *... negligenza e indugio*
> *da voi per tepidezza in ben far messo,*[376]

But an indication of *amor del bene scemo di suo dover*,[377] and another of *mal tardato remo*,[378] and a yet another of *lento amore in lui veder... o a lui ac-*

---

[374]*Dolce mio padre*...: Italian for "'Say, my sweet Father, what delinquency is purged here in the circle where we are? Although our feet may pause, pause not thy speech.' And he to me: 'The love of good, remiss in what it should have done, is here restored; here plied again the ill-belated oar; but still more openly to understand.'" (Longfellow's translation.)

[375]*Se lento amore*...: Italian for "If languid love to look on this attract you, or in attaining unto it, this cornice, after just penitence, torments you for it." (Longfellow's translation.) *Purgatory*, XVII 130-2.

[376]*Negligenza e indugio*...: Italian for "sloth and negligence you showed in doing good half-heartedly." (Longfellow's translation.)

[377]*Amor del bene*...: Italian for "Love of the good, lacking in its duty." *Purgatory*, XVII 85-6.

[378]*Mal tardato remo*...: Italian for "[the] ill-retarded oar." *Purgatory*, XVII 87.

quistare,[379] could be enough. It is not like this that love is determined in its three kinds and appellations, too abandoned to a good that is not felicity. We immediately understand what is under discussion; but in the poetic fiction Dante needed, and for this reason we needed, to want to experience difficulty.

> *Altro ben è che non fa l'uom felice;*
> *non è felicità, non è la buona*
> *essenza, d'ogni ben frutto e radice.*
>
> *L'amor ch'ad esso troppo s'abbandona,*
> *di sopra noi si piange per tre cerchi,*
> *ma, come tripartito si ragiona,*
>
> *tacciolo, acciocchè tu per te ne cherchi.*[380]

What to say? Must we say that Dante has changed system? Must we say that this love for the good that is not felicity, as much to say incontinence, does not include the three sins that remain, in other words avarice, gluttony, and lust?

Dante himself shows us clearly what we would say poorly, if we were to say it, because gradually he informs us of the name of the three offenses (*del tutto avara*, XIX 113; *avarizia*, ib. 121;

---

[379]*Lento amore...*: Italian for "listless love to look at it... or to acquire it." *Purgatory* XVII 130-1.

[380]*Altro ben è...*: Italian for "There's other good that does not make man happy; 'tis not felicity, 'tis not the good essence, of every good the fruit and root. The love that yields itself too much to this above us is lamented in three circles; but how tripartite it may be described, I say not, that thou seek it for thyself." (Longfellow's translation.) *Purgatory* XVII 133-9.

d'avarizia, XX 82; *avaro Mida*, XX 106; *avarizia, XXII* 23; *avaro*, ib. 32: *avarizia*, ib. 34; *dismisura* – (*nullo spendio con misura ferci*, Inf., VII 42) – ib. 35; *l'avarizia*, ib. 53; *la gola oltra misura*, XXIII 65: *colpe della gola*, XXIV 128; *lussuria*, XXVI 42; *Soddoma*, ib. 40, ib. 79).[381] In the same way, in Hell, Virgil categorizes three sins with one philosophical definition: three sins in Hell, three in Purgatory; in the former, bestiality and malice, but as I have demonstrated that bestiality is one of the three kinds of malice, malice then; in the latter incontinence, while the other three already mentioned by their proper names have also their theoretical grouping; three in Hell: lust, gluttony, avarice grouped together under the name of incontinence; three in Purgatory: pride, envy, and ire, grouped together under the name of triform love of evil, or malice.

In between these two ternaries is, in Hell and in Purgatory, a sin less clearly expressed which however in v. 132 of the XVIIIth canto of *Purgatory* is ultimately called: *acedia.*

But first, besides the *negligenza e indugio* born of *tepidezza*,[382] to understand or nearly the acedia punished in Ante-Purgatory, love is declared listless *a lui vedere* and *a lui acquistare*,[383] which shows the distinction between the acedia punished in Hell in

---

[381]*Avarizia... gola... lussuria...*: Italian for "avarice, gluttony, lust."

[382]*Negligenza e indugio... tepidezza*: Italian for "slothfulness and delay... listlessness."

[383]*A lui vedere... a lui acquistar*: Italian for "to look at it... to acquire it." "It" in this case being "un bene," a good.

an active life and that in a contemplative one.

In conclusion, we repeat that, just as in Purgatory, having called incontinence *Amor ch'ad esso troppo s'abbandona*,[384] and having said that it is divided into three sins not named however, does not prevent these three sins from being avarice precisely and its opposite, gluttony and lust; so too in Hell, not having spoken of malice except that it is divided into three sins, without giving the name of those three sins, does not prevent them from being precisely ire, envy, and pride.

But in *Purgatory* the three sins without a name are then given names. And in the *Inferno*? In the *Inferno* they are not given names, no; save some more-or-less clear hint. A very clear hint:

O cieca cupidigia, o ira folle,[385]

said precisely in reference to violence or bestiality (*Inf.*, XII 49); to which hint, many others are added in its place. But it could be said that Dante here pretends to be confused and wants to confuse the reader, calling Vanni Fucci and Capaneus proud, for example, who are however clearly guilty of envy and ire, the first, and of ire, the second. And here we must suppose, and are uncertain whether to speak or remain silent, some profound reason, because here is above all, I believe, the originality of Dante's theologico-pe-

---

[384]*Amor ch'ad esso...*: Italian for "Love that abandons itself too much to it." *Purgatory*, XVII 136.

[385]*O cieca cupidigia...*: Italian for "O blind cupidity, or mad ire." *Inferno*, XII 49.

nal system; the two-bodied Minotaur is really mad
anger, without reason, and the three-bodied Geryon
and Lucifer are the two sins that contain three elements, that is, in addition to will and appetite, reason
as well. Lucifer is clearly pride itself: how is Geryon
not envy? But I don't want to repeat myself. One
must keep this in mind above all, that Dante, in order
to conceive of or define sins, has before him, besides
Aristotle, besides Saint Thomas Aquinas, *Genesis*.
Proud is, to him, anyone who similar to Lucifer, rebellious before God; to Adam, disobedient before
God; to Cain, the fratricide. Envious is anyone who
reminds him of Cain, not in the sense of the family
circle, but in the larger circle of humanity; guilty of
anger is Adam, Cain, *Man,* who alone with *heart,* that
is with *desire (l'una parte chiamo cuore, ciò è l'appetito:*[386] *Vita Nova* cap. XXXVIII), without recourse
to reason, gets upset with other men, with himself,
and with God who gave him the benefit of life, which
he takes for a punishment, and the punishment of procreation and labor, which he takes for an injustice.

5.

I summarize from Bartoli's book. Minich holds that
Dante had *sketched out* a system of punition in the
first seven cantos, which he abandoned in the eighth,
thus giving to the Divine Comedy *those vast propor-
tions* that we admire in it. Todeschini confutes this
hypothesis *as not very honorable to Alighieri's literary reputation*. Bartoli admits that *even after that*

---

[386]*L'una parte chiamo...*: Italian for "the one part I call heart, that
is, desire."

confutation, certain difficulties remain.

Page 53:

*In such abundance of sin, we feel that
something here is missing: three of the
capital vices are missing, pride, envy,
and acedia. Let's start with acedia...*

I summarize again. Bartoli does not believe
that the apathetic reside in the vestibule of Hell, nor
that the Poet confounds acedia with sloth, with the
cowardice of the soul.

Page 55:

*Although I cannot conceal that an ar-
gument in favor of the opinion held by
Daniello and others whom I have cited
would be this, that acedia is punished
in Dante's Purgatory in a way that is
analogical to how cowards are punished in the Ante-Inferno. They are
condemned to running about perpetually behind pennons; and even those
who atone for the sin of acedia have to
run about as punishment:*

> … correndo
> Si movea tutta quella turba magna[387]
> – *Purg.*, XVIII 97-8.

Noi siam di voglia a muoverci sì pieni

---

[387]*Correndo si movea...*: Italian for "all that large crowd moved,
running."

che ristar non potem...[388]
– ib. 115-16

The argument put forward here is decisive for me; but it is necessary to fill it out and clarify it. Acedia, which is listless love in the seeing or acquiring of the good; which is, in other words, contained in the contemplative life just as in the active life (even this ordering, first the contemplative, then the active, is not random, as we will see); double acedia then, spiritual and bodily, is punished by Dante in two ways, with the forced mobility of whoever wants or would want to stay put, with the forced immobility of whoever would want instead to act now. In fact, the Poet found the way to unite these two castigations into one. Let us break down the whole into parts.

The indolent of the Ante-Inferno run about perpetually, but in the vestibule of Hell where *the envious of every other sort* even would want to enter! In the Stygian bog some quarrel incessantly, others are thick in the mud: both *cry* and *grow sad* and would like to leave from that place, at the cost of entering Dis even. The spiritually apathetic in Limbo calm down naturally but sigh, although their laments do not sound like woes; and they live in a continual desire without hope. The spiritually apathetic in the *cemetery* on the terraces of Dis, who are similar in so many ways to the *gente di molto valore... che in quel limbo eran sospesi*,[389] given that in the cemetery there are magnanimous people, with whom to speak and whom listening to is a valid desire; these other apathetic

---

[388]*Noi siam di voglia*...: Italian for "We are so full of desire to move that we cannot stay."

souls who, instead of sighs, let out strong laments,

che ben parean di miseri e d'offesi,[390]

are buried in sarcophagi that will be closed forever on the day of Universal Judgment. These are the castigations of acedia in Hell. And in Purgatory the apathetic in part are

> *... anime che movieno i piè...*
> *e non parevan, sì venivan lente;*
>
> *... persone*
> *che si stavan all'ombra dietro al sasso,*
> *com'uom per negligenza a star si pone.*
>
> *ed un di lor, che mi sembrava lasso,*
> *sedeva ed abbracciava le ginocchia,*
> *tenendo il viso giù tra esse basso;*[391]

they are *people* who

> *venivan... innanzi a noi un poco,*

---

[389]*Gente di molto valore*...: Italian for "people of great merit who were suspended in that limbo." *Inferno*, IV 44-45.

[390]*Che ben parean*...: Italian for "who appear quite miserable and tormented." *Inferno* IX, 123.

[391]*Anime che movieno*...: Italian for "souls, that moved their feet in our direction, and did not seem to move, they came so slowly... persons... who in the shadow stood behind the rock, as one through indolence is wont to stand. And one of them, who seemed to me fatigued, was sitting down, and both his knees embraced, holding his face low down between them bowed." (Longfellow's translation.) *Purgatory*, III 59-60, 103-18.

cantando Miserere *a verso a verso,*[392]

they are souls that *sit* singing in the pleasant valley. And it is not desire that they are lacking; but hope, without also being annulled as with the suspended in Limbo whom they are similar to (there, little children, who died on the sill of life; here, wicked men who repent on the sill of death; there, *spiriti magni* in a noble castle; here, an *esercito gentile*[393] in a pleasant valley), hope circumscribes them. He, who showed

> *... sé più negligente*
> *che se pigrizia fosse sua sirocchia,*[394]

who has such *lazy movements* and such *short sentences*, says:

> *... Frate, l'andare in su che porta?*
> *chè non mi lascerebbe ire ai martiri*
> *l'uccel* [sic] *di Dio che siede in su la porta;*[395]

that if it were not so, oh! they would run fast those

---

[392]*Venivan... innanzi a noi...*: Italian for "slightly ahead of us... approached, singing the *Miserere* verse after verse." *Purgatory*, V 23-4.

[393]*Spiriti magni... esercito gentile*: Italian for "great spirits... a noble army."

[394]*Sé più negligente...*: Italian for "himself more negligent still than if laziness itself were his sister." *Purgatory*, IX 110-1.

[395]*Frate, l'andare...*: Italian for "brother, what's the use of climbing? Since to my torment would not let me go the Angel of God, who sitteth at the gate." (Longfellow's translation.) *Purgatory*, IV 127-129.

souls, like the *masnada fresca:*[396]

> *Come quando, cogliendo biada o loglio,*
> *li colombi adunati alla pastura,*
> *queti senza mostrar l'usato orgoglio,*
>
> *se cosa appare ond'elli abbian paura,*
> *subitamente lasciano star l'esca*
> *perchè assaliti son da maggior cura.*[397]

Nor is the impossibility of climbing during the night without reason:

> *non però che altra cosa desse briga,*
> *che la notturna tenebra ad ir suso;*
> *quella col non poter la voglia intriga.*[398]

Which recalls, with the convenient difference and proportion between Hell and Purgatory, the tenebrae of Limbo:

> *Loco è laggiù non tristo da martiri*
> *ma di tenebre solo.*[399]

They are, as the commentators note, the evan-

---

[396]*Masnada fresca*: Italian for "fresh crowd." *Purgatory* II 130.

[397]*Come quando...*: Italian for "Even as when, collecting grain or tares, the doves, together at their pasture met, quiet, nor showing their accustomed pride, if aught appear of which they are afraid, upon a sudden leave their food alone, because they are assailed by greater care." (Longfellow's translation.) *Purgatory* II 124-129.

[398]*Non però che...*: Italian for "Not that aught else would hindrance give, however, to going up, save the nocturnal darkness; this with the want of power the will perplexes." (Longfellow's translation.) *Purgatory* VII 55-7.

gelical tenebrae (Giovanni XII 35); whoever walks in them does not know where he goes. Continuing now, besides these apathetic – slow, lazy, sedentary – souls in Purgatory, there are those, of whom Bartoli speaks, who run and are full of desire to move about; there is immobility therefore and forced mobility in Purgatory, just as there is mobility and even forced immobility in Hell, in proper order, i.e., in reverse order; as listless love has arisen with Virgil like this – *in lui vedere o a lui acquistare* – inversely, that is from the collocation of acedia in Hell; where it is first the carnality of the indolent and then the spirituality of the suspended, first the carnality of the quarrelsome and those thick in the mud and then the spirituality of those who kill the soul with the body. Nothing by chance, and all admirable, as with the works of God!

I have amplified then and clarified and completed Bartoli's argument. Yes: the apathetic are the wretched in the vestibule of Hell because condemned to the contrapasso of running perpetually, like the apathetic on the forth ledge of Purgatory; similar to the apathetic are others perpetually in motion in Hell, or those who

> *si percotean, non pur con mano*
> *ma con la testa, col petto e co' piedi,*
> *troncandosi coi denti a brano a brano.*[400]

---

[399]*Loco è laggiù...*: Italian for "A place there is below not sad with torments, but darkness only." (Longfellow's translation.) *Purgatory* VII 28-9.

[400]*Si percotean...*: Italian for "smote each other not alone with hands, but with the head and with the breast and feet, tearing each other piecemeal with their teeth.." (Longfellow's translation.) *Inferno*, VII 112-4.

To whom, also grouped together in castigation, are other apathetic souls who however are condemned to immobility; in the same way as a diverse proportion of apathetic souls are condemned to absolute or relative immobility, without hope or with limited hope, with a desire that either cannot be fulfilled or can be, but only after a certain period of time, an ardent desire however, shrouded in total or partial, real or symbolic, darkness; those who were suchlike with respect to the spiritual life: the suspended in Limbo, the buried in sarcophagi, the slow and lazy on the mountain, the seated in the valley.

Page 56:

As for believing then the apathetic punished in the black, liquid slurry, I would say firmly that it is impossible.

About which Bartoli gives some reasons which it is pointless to combat with other arguments. Enough has already been said about it.

Dante says:

sotto l'acqua ha gente che sospira,
e fanno pullular quest'acqua al summo come l'occhio ti dice, u' che s'aggira.

Fitti nel limo dicon: "Tristi fummo nell'aer dolce che del sol s'allegra, portando dentro accidioso *fummo:*

> *or ci attristiam nella belletta negra.*
> *Quest'inno si gorgolian nella strozza,*
> *chè dir nol posson con parola integra."[401]*

Gregory of Nyssa, cited in St. Thomas' *Summa* (1st of the 2nd, XXXV 8), says *Acedia is the sadness that cuts off the voice*. What else to look for? And it is to be noted that these people *sigh* as well, like those in Limbo, and like those in the sarcophagi which the *dolorous* souls leave to sigh.

Page 59:

> *This circle (the 5th) of Dante's Hell is the place where many interpreters lump all the sins that they are unable to find elsewhere. What is lacking is the punishment of acedia, envy, and pride: and yet, they say, given these must be there, let's look for them in the fifth circle.*

To be honest, THEY MUST BE THERE. But come on: let us admit the *possibility* that Dante didn't forget or that after the 7th canto, having changed system, he neglected nothing less than the most grievous capital sins, envy and pride (acedia is out of question). Let us

---

[401]*Sotto l'acqua*...: Italian for "Beneath the water people are, who sigh and make this water bubble at the surface, as the eye tells thee wheresoe'er it turns. Fixed in the mire they say, 'We sullen were in the sweet air, which by the sun is gladdened, bearing within ourselves the sluggish reek; now we are sullen in this sable mire.' This hymn do they keep gurgling in their throats, for with unbroken words they cannot say it." (Longfellow's translation.) *Inferno*, VII 118-126.

admit this possibility; but let us admit also the possibility that pride and envy are there. Inquirers into the *Divine Comedy* were right to look for them, but they made two mistakes:

1st, to have sought them in the filthy bog;

2nd, not to have sought a third sin, which is missing, together with the other two, and which is not acedia, and which together with the other two is called *spiritual*, which is strictly united with the other two, which together with the other two Dante made descend, in *Purgatory,* from the *amor del male,*[402] and that it is for this reason that they needed to search for it together with the other two. There were two small words – *vinse l'ira*[403] – which all the commentators kept external to the true mode of interpreting the moral construction of the *Comedy*.

The souls of those whom anger overcame, how are they not the iracund? Thus did everyone think, and they were deceived. And yes, Dante proposes to us a knot, an *enigma forte*; but he already told us how to solve it and explain it. Whoever reins in *anger* is, for him, continent and temperate; whoever does not rein it in, who lets himself be taken by the hand, whoever is *overcome* by it is incontinent and intemperate: by irascibility, to be clear. Now, incontinence is not malice. But the capital sin anger is the sin of malice, as Dante makes clear in *Purgatory*:

---

[402] *Amor del male*: Italian for "love of evil."

[403] *Vinse l'ira*: Italian for "anger overcame." (Longfellow's translation.) *Inferno*, VII 116.

... esso amor

(of evil)

nasce in tre modi in vostro limo,[404]

by way of anger, envy, and pride. Therefore, in
Dante, incontinence of anger is not really the sin of
anger. This goes hand in hand with the harm done to
one's neighbor, to at least one's neighbor: I say "at
least" because in the offense of anger that is atoned
for in the second realm, it cannot be hatred of self and
hatred of God: with harm, therefore, to someone else.
Now, Dante expressly says this about Filippo Argenti,
that he

in sé medesmo si volgea co' denti.[405]

And he does not have to tell us what his mis-
deed was, but says only:

Quei fu al mondo persona orgogliosa;
Bontà non è *che sua memoria fregi.*[406]

A bad disposition consequently and a negative
sin, an absolute lack of good works. This sinner resembles the indolent then

---

[404]*Esso amor nasce...*: Italian for "this love is born in three ways
in your clay." *Purgatory*, XVII 113-4.

[405]*In sé medesmo...*: Italian for "turned on himself with his teeth."
Inferno, VIII 63.

[406]*Quei fu al mondo...*: Italian for "He was an arrogant person in
the world; he is not remembered for his goodness." *Inferno*, VIII
46-7.

che visser senz'infamia e senza lodo,[407]

whose

fama... il mondo esser non lassa;[408]

who

mai non fur vivi.[409]

The former had no will, the latter subjugated it to their desire, in other words to that part of themselves which is called irascibility; but neither the one nor the other did evil or good. They are the apathetic, both of them. So the interpreters would have concluded, unless they had let themselves be led astray by the word *anger*, which Dante attributed to malice! So the interpreters would have concluded, thinking that, because anger is the sin of malice, Dante would have attributed the harm done by someone who was punished for anger similarly to how he attributes it with respect to others punished for malice. Whereas he can but narrate or have narrated a particular sin of the offenders of incontinence, as he did for Francesca, he can only hint at their habitual vice, as he did for Cleopatra and Ciacco and the avaricious. To the apathetic then, or rather the incontinent and those lacking in irascibility (they are of two types, the quarrelsome

---

[407]*Che visser...*: Italian for "who lived with neither infamy nor praise." *Inferno*, III 36.

[408]*Fama di loro* ...: Italian for "fame... is not left in the world." *Inferno*, III 49.

[409]*Mai non fur vivi*: Italian for "never were alive." *Inferno*, III 64.

and those thick in the mud: we have spoken about them multiple times), he had better reasons for abstaining from attributing concrete deeds. They are punished *for not acting*; that is, they are apathetic for not having acted; for not having dominated or used their anger, or irascibility, they are incontinent. They are not guilty then of an evil act committed against their neighbor or against themselves, or that they intended to commit against God: and for that reason they are not perpetrators of ire. And the interpreters would have taken a different approach after this. They would no longer have sought out the other two sins, envy and pride, in the bog, because according to the declaration in Purgatory, they were never dissociated by harm done to their neighbor. They come, the first group, out of fear of losing power, favor, honor, and fame, and the second group out of desire for excellence; but both, the one out of fear, the other out of hope, need the *neighbor* to be suppressed and the *others* not to rise above them. The interpreters then would have examined by whom and in what place Dante recounted or hinted at an act or actions of suppression of one's *neighbor* or of *others*, and would have said that in that place both pride and envy was punished; as most certainly they would have concluded that anger was punished where vengeance was reported. They would have, in any case, turned their back on the fertile bog, because it would have appeared impossible to them that of the three sins that are born of the love of evil and that are manifest in the harm done to one's neighbor (at the least, one's neighbor), – that it was not said about them but that:

Bontà non è che lor memoria fregi.

And here I anticipate an objection.

The souls in the mud torment themselves as is recounted in Dante, and they do themselves as much harm as they can. That is in contradiction to what one might infer from the verse:

in sè medesmo si volgea co' denti.

To which I respond, first of all, that the evil they do to themselves is understood as done by themselves to themselves and is significative of the ill will that they had in life, the which did not even manifest itself as injury in life. In death, yes, it manifests itself, in their punishment. What appear as big insects and wasps to the indolent, goading the deceased into an activity which they did not exhibit in life, are to these other souls who are indolent of evil, those who were continually led to do harm to their neighbor, their companions' torment. With just how much adroitness and profundity that was thought out by Dante, everyone can see.

A final observation. Dante's interpreters are some of the most learned and sharp people around; first of all, I dare to mention, Isidore Del Lungo. And even he, while dazzled like others by the words *cui vinse l'ira*, can be said to agree with me, although in the Stygian bog he searches for and believes to have found, in addition to ire and acedia, envy and pride. They are there in fact, in a certain way, they are there. It can be said (and I have already said it) that in the fertile bog is punished l'*amor del male scemo di suo dovere*. Now, the love of evil is also triplicate, and, when it leads to injury, it becomes not only anger, but envy and pride as well. So that one may conclude that in the mud there truly is anger, envy, and pride, but without any effect: ill will, but apathetic.

Page 70:

Therefore, neither the apathetic, nor the proud, nor the invidious, for me, in the Styx, but only the iracund.

Therefore, neither the iracund in the Sytx, properly speaking, nor the invidious, nor the proud, but only the apathetic, apathetic like those immediately within the walls of Dis: in active life those of the Styx, in the contemplative life those within Dis; the former placed with other carnal sinners, of incontinence, the latter with other spiritual sinners, of malice: apathetic like those on either side of the Acheron: in active life the indolent, in contemplative life the suspended; and apathetic like them of course, but with one difference: those around Dis are apathetic with malevolence, those around the Acheron are such either without or against their will. Against their will, the suspended, but up to a certain point. Virgil says in *Purgatory* (III 40 ff)

E disiar vedeste senza frutto
tai, che sarebbe lor disio quetato
ch'eternalmente è dato lor per lutto.

Io dico d'Aristotile e di Plato
e di molti altri. E qui chinò la fronte,

e più non disse, e rimase turbato.[410]

He remained disturbed, thinking not only about the eternal battle of vain desire, but also recognizing that their lack of faith was voluntary. They could have believed in the coming Christ, and saved themselves.

6.

From page 70 to 75, Bartoli refers to and confutes the systems of Todeschini and Witte, wherein sinners are not distinct "according to diverse passions that push men toward sin, but chose instead the design of drawing a distinction between the effective and so-called material nature of the sins committed by them, etc., etc." It is pointless to follow Todeschini in the exposition of his system because, based on the evidence, it is exactly the opposite: Dante divided sinners according to the diverse passions which push men toward sin.

Dido and Cleopatra are not punished as suicides, nor Semiramis as incestuous, nor Francesca as an adulteress, because the passion that pushed them to sin was *amore* and *lussuria*,[411] love that is the excess

---

[410]*E disiar vedeste...*: Italian for "And ye have seen desiring without fruit, those whose desire would have been quieted, which evermore is given them for a grief. I speak of Aristotle and of Plato, and many others"; – and here bowed his head, and more he said not, and remained disturbed." (Longfellow's translation.) *Purgatory*, III 40-45.

[411]*Amore... lussuria*: Italian for "love, lust."

of good which is not good. Brunetto is not punished as a lecher, because the passion that pushed him and his companions was not the said lust or the sad love of the good, but the love of evil for which he rebelled against God the creator who commands procreation. And in the same way usurers are not punished for avarice because the passion that pushed them was also the said love of evil, for which they rebelled against God the creator and avenger, who had enjoined men to work and nourish themselves by the sweat of their brow. And so on and so forth.

> Page 72:
>
> *Witte too is of the opinion that Dante has, in the* Inferno, *punished the crime, not the passion that was the cause of the crime...*

Let us say that from time to time a vice or a sin, a habitude or an act is punished. Without looking for more, Francesca is punished for a act of love; Semiramis for a habitude, the vice of lust. But let us say also that these vices or sins are punished according to the passion that moved them. Both Semiramis' vice and Francesca's adultery were caused by the love that (for the good that was not a good) abandons itself too much to it;[412] not by the love of evil, and, as can easily be understood, not at all by *listless* love. So they are both collocated among the incontinent and among that type of theirs that is called carnal sinners.

---

[412]The love that abandons itself too much to it: *L'amor ch'ad esso troppo s'abbandona. Purgatory,* XVII 136.

Ib:

*and he cites the example of Cain, who
is in the depths of Hell not for envy,
but because he killed his brother...*

Cain is an example of envy in Purgatory and
he gives his name to the extreme ring around the ice.
He is, for Dante, guilty of pride and envy, or somewhere between pride and envy. Cain offended his
neighbor, who was also his only brother. As the aggressor of his neighbor, he violates the commandment
of the second tablet of God – not to kill; as the aggressor of his brother, the other [commandment], also
of the second [tablet], but the first, so that it is considered by theologians as similar to the those of the first;
that which enjoins reverence, as for one's parents, so
too for all one's blood relatives. As the aggressor of
one's neighbor he is envious; as the aggressor of his
brother he is proud; but, I repeat, the neighbor is reduced to his brother and the brother was his only
neighbor.

Ib.:

*and the example of Capaneus, not
punished as being proud, but as being
violent against God.*

But Capaneus is punished as being violent
against God, which is as much to say for having
wished to wreck vengeance against God himself, with
his *heart* only, in other words without intellect and

with the same irascible appetite, over and above *ill will*. He is guilty of ire, of mad ire, of that which is possessed by

> *chi spregiando Dio col* cuor *favella.*[413]

Page 73:

> *And from this long discourse of ours, what conclusion can be drawn however? This only, in my opinion: that the moral order of the first part of the Inferno presents (for whatever reasons) insurmountable difficulties.*

Unsurmountable to be sure, if one should continue to hold *color cui vinse l'ira* to be guilty of ire.

Page 74:

> *O if it were true, at least in part, the hypothesis by Minich, or if its opposite were true, we do not clearly see how Dante had conceived of the distribution of sinners punished from the second to the fifth circle, nor do we fully understand the connection between the system followed in the first seven cantos and that in the successive ones.*

It seems clear to me how Dante had conceived of that distribution, and I mean the connection be-

---

[413]*Chi sporegiando...*: Italian for "whoever disdains God *passionately.*"

tween the system of the first and that of successive cantos, which are precisely one system.

Ib.:

The fact remains that guilty passions are punished in the first seven cantos, which passions push men to sin, but that among those guilty passions three are missing, and the most fundamental ones.

The passions impelling someone to sin, in Dante, are three: love of the good which is not good, listless love of that good, love of evil. To the first corresponds incontinence, to the last malice and bestiality. As for the passion in the middle, which is negative, Dante places it in part with incontinence, in part with malice, if one observes that the people in the mud (apathetic in active life) are outside of Dis, that is incontinent, incontinent in irascibility; and the heresiarchs (apathetic in contemplative life) are within Dis, that is malicious.

Ib.:

The fact remains that, in successive cantos, what is punished more than the special passion, impelling to sin, is sin itself.

But, no: Brunetto and the others are not among the lechers, even if the sin *itself* be that of lust; the usurers and the simonists are not among the avaricious, even if the sin itself be that of avarice, as Bartoli then notes for the simonists. But for these last, and so as not to repeat myself with respect to the usurers, I point out that their impelling passion was not avarice, whatever we might think: Dante thought that the plan was to *calcare i buoni e sollevare i pravi*:[414] envy.

Ib.:

And when we are about to enter into the seventh circle, where tyrants and homicides are punished, the Poet exclaims:

> Oh cieca cupidigia, oh ira folle
> Che sì ci sproni nella vita corta,
> E nell'eterna poi sì mal c'immolle![415]

So cupidity and ire were the passions that moved homicides and tyrants; however these were not punished in the fourth and fifth circles, but in the seventh.

Pointing out that the cupidity here is not, evidently, that of money, but of vengeance, or of *evil* in general, we must express our homage of admiration

---

[414]*Calcare i buoni...*: Italian for "kick down the good and raise up the depraved."

[415]*Oh cieca cupidigia...*: Italian for "O blind cupidity, O mad ire, that spurs us on in our short lives, and then immolates us so completely in the eternal!" (Longfellow's translation.) *Inferno*, 12 49-51.

here for the subtle and profound genius of the great, extinct man. Yes: he intuited the truth, and without the obstacle of having assigned the fifth circle to ire, he would have discovered the secret of the moral construction of the *Comedy*. Because actually it is for ire that the homicides and tyrants are punished, and with them the suicides, the blasphemers, the sodomites and the usurers: for ire, which is *mad*, because they sin only with the heart or with irascible appetite, in addition to *mal volere*, but without the intervention of reason.

Page 82:

The second part of the Inferno opens with the city of Dis, around which lies the Stygian bog, outside of it; within it are the inflamed sepulchers of the Epicureans and the heretics; and this is the sixth circle, and the first of the four contained within the city of Dis.

It is the sixth circle, but just a little lower than the fifth, though not at the same level. In fact, Dante has in mind the fortifications of a real city, representing those of Dis; and the tombs are at the foot of them, in expansive fields; and these internal fields are certainly more elevated than the foundation and also than the edge of the *high, external ditches*. The disconsolate land is however inside, in the valley, but dominates it. Now, Dante wanted it like this because he wanted the heresiarchs [to be] guilty of malice, and for that reason he put them inside Dis, but he made them guilty of acedia, placing them together at the same, or nearly the same, level as the people in the mud. It is not to be passed over that Todeschini, whom Bartoli cites in a note on this point, intuited correctly when he wrote that Dante intentionally "in his work, in order to put aside certain superficial, and I would say almost material, correspondences," placed "the souls who were lost for a non-malicious lack of faith in the first circle of upper Hell because they were in correspondence with the reprobates who lacked proper faith on account of their malice, and who came to be placed by him in the first circle of lower Hell." Whence Del Lungo deduced this correspondence:

less guilty	- indolent and neutral angels (in the vestibule) - unbaptized and virtuous pagans (in the first circle)
more guilty	- Epicureans and heresiarchs (in the 6th circle) - giants (between the 8th and 9th)

Naturally, however, there are observation and distribution in the both of them. Which will become evident to whoever puts his mind to the following correspondence that I present:

acedia	involuntary in life (active, contemplative)	outside	- all hell – totally apathetic - all hell – unbaptized - deep hell – apathetic of evil
	voluntary in life (active, contemplative)	inside	- all hell – unbaptized - deep hell – apathetic of evil - deep hell – heresiarchs

Now, these are not "superficial, and I would almost say material, correspondences," but rather refer to theological dogmas for which the disorder of the things of the spirit is more serious than that of the things of the body. Nor must one forget that the fault, malicious and not malicious, of the baptized and those who kill the soul with the body, is acedia, because every ignorance is reducible to acedia. And one must remember that the fault of the unbaptized is involuntary, but only up to a certain point.

This examination can suffice. I certainly won't tarry any longer over the argument of bestiality, which I have demonstrated to be violence. Only, I will put forward an objection that I foresee. And it is this: however did it happen that the sins of the first seven cantos did not have divisions, and those of the remaining cantos have so many, bestiality or violence or anger being divided into three sins, and of these the first two divided into two more, and the third into three; simple fraud or envy into ten, complex fraud or betrayal or pride into four? My answer is that already even in the first four sins there are divisions; acedia being of four types: carnal or spiritual, without or against (in part) will and voluntary; lust being punished like love (in excess) or vice; avarice being an evil in giving or in possessing. But it is clear, even from the number of cantos that treat of these ones or those ones which describe the others, that this reason is not sufficient. The real reason lies in the nature of root causes attributed by Dante, following Aristotle, to all sins: incontinence, that is, and malice. I will get straight to the point: to everyone who accepts for a moment the superposition that Dante made of the

triple Aristotelian division onto the septenary theological distinction, there appears homogeneity, so to
speak, and uniformity in the sins of incontinence
compared to those of malice. All the more so as
Dante, taking the first human drama recounted in the
Bible for a model and type, reduced some of their
forms to lust and avarice, the which however are re-
founded in the very sin of incontinence when penitence has canceled out the *injury* or malicious purpose
of it.

IV.
Moralium Dogma.

For the extraordinary importance that this work holds
with respect to Dante's ethic, I recall here, more dis-
tinctly than in the text of the Prolegomena, some of
Sundby's tract on "Brunetto Latini" (Florence, 1884).
From p. 401, the following table is useful to meditate
on:

IUSTITIAE

	opponuntur duo	
Negligentia		Truculentia
		Vis. Fraus.

And this table is illustrated on p. 426 ff. with
words imperfectly derived from *De Officiis* (1, 7, 23).

> *Duobus praefatis iustitiae generibus*
> *totidem sunt opposita iniustitiae gen-*
> *era, quae summopere cavere oportet,*
> *scilicet truculentia et negligentia. Est*
> *truculentia iniustitia iniustam inferens*

iniuriam. Negligentia vero est non propulsare iniuriam quum possis et debeas. Est autem negligentia severitati contraria, contra ponuntur enim defendere et defensionem contemnere. Similiter truculentia liberalitati repugnat: repugnant enim beneficium dare et iniuriam irrogare... Dividitur autem truculentia in vim et fraudem: fraus quasi vulpeculae, vis quasi leonis videtur: utrumque ab homine alienissimum, sed fraus odio digna maiore...

It is clear why Dante destined the *gran regi* for the fertile bog. They were guilty of *negligentia*. And it is also clear why the just kings of the Eagle in Jove rebuke the kings for their *dispregi*, for their *viver molle*, for their lack of *valore*, for their *viltate*.

Let us read for a moment, from the book, these words, also taken from Cicero:

P. 411. Dividitur autem iustitia in severitatem et liberalitatem. Severitas est virtus debito supplicio cohibens iniuriam....

Cavenda tamen est maxime ira in puniendo, cum qua nemo tenebit mediocritatem quae est inter nimium et parum.

In the river of blood are such kings as do not

look at each other for the *ira in puniendo*.

It is useful again to meditate on this other passage, which illustrates passages in the *Comedy* and the *Convivio* and the *Epistles*:

> *Huius (magnanimitatis) officium sic monstrat Philosophus (Cic. 1, 19, 65): Magnanimi sunt habendi, non qui faciunt, sed qui propulsant iniuriam. Idcirco (1, 20, 68) ista fit in hac virtute cautela avaritiae. Non enim est consentaneum, qui metu non potest frangi, eum frangi cupiditate, nec qui invictum se a labore praestiterit, eum vinci a voluptate...*

And to illustrate the important phrase *cui vinse l'ira*, let us recall that these lines by Horace are reported in the book *Satire* with respect to temperance (p. 441):

> *Qui non moderabitur* irae
> *Infectum volet esse, dolor quod suaserit et mens.*
> Ira furor brevis est: animum *rege, qui nisi paret,*
> *Imperat: hunc frenis, hunc tu compesce catenis.*

The *animus* is also that which Dante calls *appetito* in both the *Convivio* and the *Comedy*: that which a well-tempered man must frankly sit astride using reins and spurs.

And in this small book Dante found a verse and a half by Juvenal, who gave him, by chance or not, some outline of his figuration of Geryon, the

symbol of Envy. Earlier, I also quote some passage
from this verse, because it is of equal importance:

> *Totius enim iniustitiae nulla pestis*
> *capitalior quam eorum qui tunc,*
> *maxime quum fallunt, id agunt, ut viri*
> *boni videantur (gli ipocriti tristi). Hor-*
> *atius idcirco dicit: Numquam te fallant*
> *animi sub vulpe latentes. Iuvenalis:*
> Hispida *membra quidem et* durae per
> brachia setae. *Promittunt atrocem ani-*
> *mum. id.* Fronti nulla fides.

It is superfluous to recall Geryon's hairy paws
and face of a just man.

Other Books by the Publisher

Fanchette's Pretty Little Foot by Restif de La Bretonne

Je M'Accuse... by Léon Bloy

My Hospitals & My Prisons by Paul Verlaine

Salvation Through the Jews by Léon Bloy

Words of a Demolitions Contractor by Léon Bloy

Cellulely by Paul Verlaine

Ecclesiastical Laurels by Jacques Rochette de la Morlière

Flowers of Bitumen by Émile Goudeau

Songs for Her & Odes in Her Honor by Paul Verlaine

On Huysmans' Tomb by Léon Bloy

Ten Years a Bohemian by Émile Goudeau

The Soul of Napoleon by Léon Bloy

Blood of the Poor by Léon Bloy

Joan of Arc and Germany by Léon Bloy

A Platonic Love by Paul Alexis

The Revealer of the Globe: Christopher Columbus & His Future Beatification (Part One) by Léon Bloy

An Immodest Proposal by Dr. Helmut Schleppend

The Pornographer by Restif de La Bretonne

Style (Theory and History) by Ernest Hello

On the Threshold of the Apocalypse: 1913-1915 by Léon Bloy

She Who Weeps (Our Lady of La Salette) by Léon Bloy

The Sylph by Claude Prosper Jolyot de Crébillon (*fils*)

Voyage in France by a Frenchman by Paul Verlaine

Ourigan, Oregon by William Clark, Richard Robinson, and anonymous

Drowning by Yu Dafu

Cull of April by Francis Vielé-Griffin

The Misfortune of Monsieur Fraque by Paul Alexis

Fêtes Galantes & Songs Without Words by Paul Verlaine

Joys by Francis Vielé-Griffin

The Son of Louis XVI by Léon Bloy

Septentrion by Jean Raspail

The Resurrection of Villiers de l'Isle-Adam by Léon Bloy

Poems Saturnian by Paul Verlaine

The Biography of Léon Bloy: Memories of a Friend by René Martineau

Fredegund, France: A Book of Poetry by Richard Robinson

The Good Song by Paul Verlaine

Swans by Francis Vielé-Griffin

Constantinople and Byzantium by Léon Bloy

Enamels and Cameos by Théophile Gautier

Four Years of Captivity in Cochons-sur-Marne: 1900-1904 by Léon Bloy